Give God the Glory!

Called to be

Light

in the Workplace

Testimonials and praise across the country for
Give God the Glory!

"*Give God the Glory! Called to be LIGHT in the Workplace* is a nice blend of spiritual and practical wisdom about being the best ambassador for Christ in the workplace. I especially like the servant leader section and the material about being an effective communicator. Readers will be stirred to press on toward the mark to win the prize (i.e. Christ) for which are call called heavenward. Mr. Johnson challenges our complacency and encourages us to maintain a "new wineskin heart" into which our Lord can pour much of the "new wine" that is found in this book."

—Jim Biscardi, Jr., President,
New Jersey Christian Ministries, Inc.

"Many authors write about surviving and thriving in the workplace. There have also been many books written on being a Christian light. However, few if any books have effectively integrated these two important topics into an inspiring and very useful book. Mr. Johnson is successful in this endeavor. His new work is very meaningful in a challenging and chaotic work environment. He challenges employees to be Christian lights on their respective jobs. Through a comprehensive analysis of the Bible and the three phases of career progression, Mr. Johnson reminds employees that God is in the workplace."

—Diane Floyd Sutton, President,
Sutton Enterprises, Washington, DC
*Author of **Increasing the Spirit and***
Effectiveness of People in the Workplace

"Simplistically clear and incisive, a real need for the 21st century working world."

—*Melvin Johnson, Sr., Founder and Pastor, True Disciple Ministries, Somerville, New Jersey*

"In my professional role as editor, book coach, and author of five of my own books, I am immensely impressed with Brother Kevin Johnson's latest work, **Give God the Glory!** *Called to be LIGHT in the Workplace.* Not only is the content of the book especially helpful to me as a leader who has mentored many women over the past 25 years, but the structure of the book is outstanding. The quotes, graphics and illustrations are excellent. Above all, I appreciate to that which he has presented as possible solutions to our day-to-day challenges in the workplace. Taking one of his personal quotes from the book, let me say this: 'Excellence never happens by accident. We have to make it happen.' Kevin has made it happen with his latest educational tool. It needs to be on every employer's shelf."

—*Minister M.D. Edwards, Founder and President, The Called and Ready Writers, Detroit, Michigan*

"Kevin's knowledge of the Lord and writing are incomparable to anyone I've met in the industry, plus his spirit is so warm and open—he is a true servant of the Lord. Very inspiring!"

—*Pam Perry, President, American Christian Writers, Detroit chapter*

"You're in a store thinking about buying this book. You ask yourself two logical questions: 'Is it worth spending $15 to read what this man has to say about being a Christian in the workplace? Will I feel that I received my money's worth when I finish this book?" The answer is a resounding YES! Kevin Johnson has taken the Word of God, blended it with years of experience in government and corporations, seasoned it with helpful quotations, examples and resources, and baked it in the fire of the Holy Spirit to cook up a very relevant book. I believe that, in God's economy, the $15 you choose to invest in *Give God the Glory: Called to be LIGHT in the Workplace* can deliver a profoundly positive and eternal return-on-investment."

> —*Drew M. Crandall, President,*
> *Northeast Christians At Work*

The principle purpose—God made man for His glory! As you think of that concept, how much do we really understand what the glory of God is all about? How does the glory of God relate to our everyday life?

Kevin Johnson has presented to us how we can glorify God not only in church but also in the workplace. It is of vital importance that we grasp this principle which has been presented for us in Kevin's intriguing work called, "Give God the Glory!"

May this be the pursuit of all of us as we think of the very purpose God had for us as He placed us on planet Earth.

> —*Joe Jordan, Executive Director,*
> *Word of Life Fellowship, Inc.,*
> *Schroon Lake, New York*

Give God the Glory!

Called to be *Light* in the Workplace

Kevin Wayne Johnson

Writing for the Lord™ Ministries
Clarksville, Maryland 21029
www.writingforthelord.com

Give God the Glory!
Copyright © 2003 by Kevin Wayne Johnson
Second Printing

Cover Concept by Kevin Wayne Johnson
Cover Design by ES Productions, Incorporated
Somerville, New Jersey

For each book sold, $2.00 is donated to Bethany Christian Ser-
vices, a national Christian adoption and education agency for
young mothers who seek God's guidance and direction concerning
their pregnancy.

Distributed throughout the United States, Canada, and internation-
ally by:
FaithWorks, a division of the National Book Network, Inc.
9247 Hunterboro Drive
Brentwood, TN 37027
(877) 323-4550 (phone) / (877) 323-4551 (fax)
custserv@faithworksonlince.com (email)
www.faithworksonline.com

Unless otherwise noted, all scripture references are taken from the
King James Version of The Holy Bible, The New Open Bible
Study Edition, Thomas Nelson, Incorporated, 1990.

ISBN: 0-9705902-1-0
Library of Congress Catalog Number: 2002109315

Printed in the United States of America

Other books by Kevin Wayne Johnson:

Give God the Glory!
Know God & Do the Will of God Concerning Your Life

Attention corporations; institutions, colleges and universities; literary and publishing groups; civic organizations, churches and bookstores:

Quantity discounts are available in bulk purchases of this book for educational training purposes, fund-raising, or gift giving. Special books, booklets, articles, or book excerpts can also be created to fit your specific needs.

To learn details: Contact *Writing for the Lord*[TM] **Ministries** at: **(443) 535-0475 or www.writingforthelord.com**

Contents

This book is dedicated to the loving memory of my mother, Adele. Mom departed this life on Sunday afternoon, March 18, 2001 at approximately 3:00pm. Mom, I thank you for your light that shined during the 62 years God placed you on this earth. Through your life, you ignited my life and encouraged me to let my light so shine before men, that they may see the goodness of God. Thank you for the memories I will always treasure and especially for the flame that burns within. I love you and your light will be with me forever...

Glory!

Glory is—A divine quality. Literally meaning "heavy" and "weighty." It includes the brightness, splendor, and radiance of God's presence; God's visible revelation of Himself.

Our word "doxology" comes from "doxa," the Greek word for Glory.

Acknowledgements

Giving thanks to God Almighty, first and foremost, I acknowledge the wonderful blessings that shower me each and everyday. I openly and unashamedly acknowledge my personal relationship with Him, through Jesus Christ– which is the sole reason for my joy, peace, and good health.

To my wife Gail, I say "Thank You," because we celebrated our 10th wedding anniversary on March 6th—the same month my second book was released. Gail, your continued support has encouraged my writing. Together, let's continue to Give God the Glory! for the remainder of our time on earth as husband and wife.

Thanks to my three sons—Kevin, Christopher, and Cameron—for being the precious boys that you are and for making me a proud Daddy. I love each of you more every day.

Thank you, Dad for your strength, especially since Mom's death, and for your voice of support. It's always comforting to hear encouraging words from your father. I appreciate all of the book sales and word-of-mouth endorsements you generated throughout the Richmond, Virginia community.

Thank you Pastor Pat, my beloved Pastor and leader, who allowed me to grow, develop, and mature so that I can be prepared to respond to my ministerial calling. Your example has spawned zeal deep within me and caused me to excel as a servant. Teaching and praying in our local church is indeed preparing me to be an effective witness on behalf of our Lord and Savior Jesus Christ.

To the Shiloh Pentecostal Church, Inc. Christian Love Center family, and especially my fellow deacons, I love you all and thank you for the fellowship. It is a labor of love. I thank Steve Gilliland for inspiring me and challenging me to write from the heart.

To all of the book editors, reviewers, bookstore owners/managers, professional associates, radio and television personalities, churches, clergy, associates, family and friends, thank you for what I have gleaned from your teachings about this industry during the last two years. Your advice, counsel, mentoring, prayers, and collective support, have made me a more effective writer for the Lord.

"Ye are the light of the world. A city that is set on a hill cannot be hid. Neither do men light a candle and put it under a bushel, but on a candlestick; and it giveth light unto all that are in the house."
(Matthew 5:14-15)

Preface

I am a Christian. I love God because at first, He loved me. He has done marvelous things for my wife and I on our respective jobs over the past 19 years and I am eternally grateful. *Give God the Glory! Called to be Light in the Workplace* is the second book in the series about God's goodness as expressed to His children in different stages of their lives.

Within these pages, based on God's Holy Word, I intend to demonstrate, that in three levels of our work life—the beginning (intern or trainee), journeyman (mid-level manager), and mentor (leadership and senior executive)—God calls Christians to be *light* at every step along the way.

I will educate each reader to recognize danger signs that Satan puts before God's children and how Christians' responses and reactions to these dangers separate them from those who choose to walk in darkness. Our *light* must shine and always be illuminated on our jobs to give others hope as well as the desire, and courage, to uphold ethical, Godly, and disciplined behavior during the 40 to 60 hours of the traditional work week. To this end, we are commissioned and called by God, through Jesus Christ, to be distinctively different and to excel at our professions. Our jobs are a resource, but as Christians, God is our performance source. As long as we stay connected to Him, we have assurance through His Word about the guarantee of peace and tranquility to achieve our dreams—*"...but with God all things are possible."* (Matthew 19:26) When God calls us to do something, He also equips us to handle the job and any challenges we will face (Romans 11:29).

When it comes to the workforce, one particular phrase that has been said many times, bears repeating: "We have more things in common than we have different." We all rely upon our skills and intellect, athleticism and body strength, charisma, and work ethic when it comes to earning a living. Simply put, we each must work to earn money and sustain ourselves during our lifetime. In the first Chapter of Genesis, Verse 26, God's first commandment to Adam was to *dress* and *keep* The Garden of Eden. Translation—Work! It was a doubly dutiful command. The Creator designed His creation to work. Even in today's world, that is the primary means by which we earn money to pay for life's necessities: shelter, clothes, food, transportation, health care, and education. Work is a necessity of life, and God's Word says: *"If you don't work, you don't eat."* (2 Thessalonians 3:10)

Our jobs can bring interesting and sometimes extremely frustrating challenges into our lives. How we choose to respond to work's never-ending challenges is the key that separates those who enjoy promotions from those who do not. Needless to say, the workplace is a very competitive environment. Most of our colleagues, bosses, subordinates, and peers at work continually seek more of everything—more money, more attractive benefits, and better opportunities—often within the organization or company where they are currently working.

When viewed with competitive eyes, you may stand in someone else's way. The competitive spirit, which is satanic, promotes self-centered behavior and is manifested outwardly at different stages of people's lives or careers. Satan is an accuser of our brethren (Revelation 12:10); is wicked (Matthew 13:9); is a deceiver (Revelation 20:10); is our adversary (1 Peter 5:8); and is the ruler of this world (Ephesians 6:12). Satan is real! Subconsciously unaware of their conduct, most people tend to think more of themselves than they do about others, without realizing the effect their behavior may have on other people.

I officially entered the workforce in the summer of 1984, following a year of disappointing unemployment. Since that time, I have survived a myriad of changes within the federal government and within corporate America. The majority of these changes have been unannounced, frequent, continual, self-serving, unproductive, detrimental to the workforce, and devastating to individuals and entire families as well.

Countless numbers of people have not been able to cope, while others are left bitter and have chosen the path of underachievement. Thus, many have failed to fulfill their God-ordained purpose during their lifetime.

In Chapters five through seven of the Book of Matthew, Jesus' first sermon during His public ministry focuses on teaching us how to live within The Kingdom of God. Jesus clearly demonstrates that there is a distinction between *how to earn a living* (how we make money to survive) and *how to live* (the persistent application of Godly principles to everyday life). In these passages of scripture, Jesus teaches His disciples and a multitude gathered at a mountain on the edge of the Sea of Galilee, about three character traits: attitude, and how to be *light* and *salt*.

History reveals this mountain is most likely northwest of Capernaum, for, shortly after this "Sermon on the Mount," we find Jesus and His disciples entering that city. These three character traits are explained in detail by Jesus, a masterful teacher, who used "parables" as object lesson(s) for the purpose of extracting a spiritual meaning from natural examples. I have always found it interesting and insightful that, during His three-and-one-half-year public ministry, Jesus would focus on character traits that can be applied to today's workforce. Even in His first message, it was as if He knew what the people needed. As students, we see it translated through His trial discourse.

What follows are God-centered and ethical principles about how to live successfully during our entire lifetime—on earth and especially within the workplace.

Now, let us *Give God the Glory!*...
Kevin Wayne Johnson

Then spake Jesus again unto them, saying, *"I am The* **Light** *of the world: he that followeth Me shall not walk in darkness, but shall have the* **light** *of life."* **(John 8: 12)**

Introduction

During my 19 years in the workforce—15 with the federal government and four within the setting of corporate America—I have seen friends, peers, associates, and colleagues, at all levels, encounter multiple problems while at work. I, too, have faced them. In most instances, the affected person feels isolated, alone, and trapped, with nowhere to turn. They are NOT alone.

Give God the Glory! *Called to be **Light** in the Workplace* exposes the challenges that *all* people face on the job. Throughout the history of this country, there has been tremendous change in the workplace. America has shifted from an agricultural society (late 1600's to 1880) to an industrial society (1890 to 1980), to an information society (1985 to present). Keeping pace with these significant changes is a full-time job in and of itself. Having a personal relationship with God, through Jesus Christ, is the assurance that we can overcome all of the pressure and change that is inherent to a typical workday.

The subtitle is the heart of this book, yet the desired objective is to fully recognize and acknowledge our responsibility to *Give God the Glory! "Called"* is defined as "My desire to do." In the original Greek language, *kaleō*, which is derived from the root *kal*, means "to call anyone, invite, summon," particularly of the divine call to partake of the blessing of redemption and of nomenclature or vocation. *Light, phōs*, derives from roots *pha–* and *phan–* in the original Greek language. In this context, man, naturally, is incapable of receiving spiritual light inasmuch as he lacks the capacity for spiritual things. Hence, believers are called 'sons of light' not merely because they have received a revelation from God, but because in the New Birth they have received the spiritual capacity for it. The word "light" is referenced in *The Holy Bible* 264 times! Light is characterized as an element that:

Illuminates	Shines
Exposes Darkness	Expels Darkness
Penetrates	Causes one to *see*
Extends Brightness	Radiates
Projects	Reveals

The *workplace* is defined as a place where people are employed; it is the work setting in general.

As a long-time employee of the federal government with a career that spans across the three stages of one's work life, I have experienced the number one problem that federal employees face: *Bureaucracy*. As a manager and director/executive within corporate America, I have experienced the number one problem that corporate employees face: *An inability to effectively communicate.* Nevertheless, I have survived by often thinking about and reciting one of my favorite spiritual songs—*"When I think of the goodness of Jesus and all He's done for me, My soul cries out Hallejuah, I thank God for saving me!"*

God has equipped each of His children with gifts that are unique and distinguishable from everyone else on earth. His Word says, *"Every good gift and every perfect gift is from above, and cometh down from the Father of **lights**, with whom is no variableness, neither* *shadow of turning."* (James 1:17) These gifts are without repentance. Further, God assures us in His Word that:

He cannot change—*"For I am the Lord, I change not…"* (Malachi 3:6),

He cannot lie—*"That by two immutable things, in which it was impossible for God to lie…"* (Hebrews 6:18) and "In hope of eternal life, which God, that cannot lie, promised before the world began" (Titus 1:2),

He is the same forever—*"Jesus Christ the same yesterday, and today, and forever"* (Hebrews 13:8),

He cannot speak empty words—*"So shall my word be that goeth forth out of my mouth: it shall not return unto me void, but it shall prosper in the things whereto I sent it,"* (Isaiah 55:11) and

He cannot break any promises—*"My covenant will I not break, nor alter the thing that is gone out of my lips."* (Psalm 89:34)

This book is systemically divided into three parts. Part One—*The Formative Years*—is intended to remind the mature worker of our humble beginnings in our respective careers. It will also encourage those entering the workforce to focus on the important things and to dismiss the unimportant. I still remember my first day at work on July 23, 1984, exactly one week after my 24th birthday, at the Defense Personnel Support Center in Philadelphia, Pennsylvania. I vividly remember my first supervisors—Mr. Delma Hughes and Mrs. Catherine Ward—as I began my classroom and on-the-job training assignments in an old government warehouse equipped with third-hand furniture that was purchased at a General Services Administration auction. There was no air conditioning to cool the stifling Philadelphia heat that permeated the setting where I worked. I still send Mrs. Ward a Christmas card every year as a sign of appreciation for showing her *light* in the midst of less-than-ideal working conditions.

As we enter the workforce and transition from growth to development to maturity, we look to peers, supervisors, and other mentors to give us advice on how to advance to the next level. Mr. Hughes and Mrs. Ward, thank you.

Part Two—*The Journeyman Years*—targets the group of workers who have learned and mastered the basic elements of the job and seek advancement into mid-level positions. During this phase, we tend to view our position as more than just a job, but a career. We find ourselves being asked to mentor others at the entry level while, at the same time, earnestly seek senior level officials to assist us with our next career move. Intelligence, tact, savvy, professionalism, integrity, balance, ethics, responsibility and accountability are the key elements to succeed at this level. It is during this stage that we transition from learning to leading and it requires more than inner drive to succeed.

The reliance upon people who God places in our paths to lead, guide and direct us—those whose trust we have earned through excellence and demonstrated potential on projects over a period of time—will also play an important role. Those who will give us enough room to make mistakes, yet protect us from less-passionate peers who salivate at opportunities to openly humiliate their subordinates for even slight errors when committed.

In 1993, God placed wonderful people in my path, who were instrumental in propelling my career development into the executive ranks. They too, are on my Christmas mailing list as a means to express my continual appreciation for their protection and to keep them apprised of my family development, overall standing and wellness.

To encourage others to reach their potential, formal leadership training is reinforced by the combined principle of application and self-motivation. Jesus taught His first disciples to *"Launch out into the deep"* (Luke 5:4) and to trust in His Word. In doing so, the fishermen, soon to be His disciples, let down their nets and caught so many fish that their nets broke! (Luke 5:6)

Part Three—*The Mentoring Years*—encourages us to reinvest time and energy into individuals. People are the human capital of any organization and the most valuable commodity in the workplace. A brief look at the lives of notable historic figures such as Evangelist Billy Graham and Dr. Martin Luther King, Jr. provide inspirational stories of how two men, raised in the southern part of the United States, taught the entire world about the importance and awesome responsibility of raising the productivity level of others. In the book of Genesis, chapter 1, verse 28, God blesses man—male and female—after creating them in His image and after His likeness. God then gave four instructions and said unto them, *"Be fruitful, multiply, and replenish the earth, and subdue it."* Through the lives of Evangelist Graham and Dr. King, we have vivid examples about how to raise the productivity level of others, as God instructs.

Caution: *"For the love of money is the root of all evil…"* (1 Timothy 6:10) Corporations thrive on their ability to make lots of money! In an era of antitrust, accounting irregularities, countless lawsuits, constant restructuring, employee layoffs, and outlandish bonuses to top executives, God can and will send a stern warning *"To humble ourselves under the mighty hand of God, that He may exalt you in due time"* (1 Peter 5:6) and *"Humble yourselves in the sight of the Lord, and He shall lift you up."* (James 4:10)

In the book of Ephesians, Chapter 5, The Apostle Paul challenges and encourages the saints at Ephesus to walk as children of *light*. He reminds them in Chapter 1, verse 3 that our Heavenly Father has blessed them with all spiritual blessings in heavenly places through Christ and that He has chosen them before the foundation of the world. Therefore, in verse 4, Paul urges them to be holy and without blame before Him in love. Today, we have the same covenant right and God is speaking to us as well. We are to be followers of God as dear children and walk in love, as Christ loved us (Ephesians, Chapter 5, verses 1 and 2). Throughout Chapter 5, Paul was inspired by God to write His instructions. Verse 8 states: *"For ye were sometimes darkness, but now are ye **light** in the Lord: walk as children of **light**."* Verse 11 states: *"And have no fellowship with the unfruitful works of darkness, but rather reprove them."* And finally, Verses 13 and

14 state: *"But all things that are reproved are made manifest by the light: for whatsoever doth make manifest is light. Wherefore he saith, AWAKE THOU THAT SLEEPEST, AND ARISE FROM THE DEAD, AND CHRIST SHALL GIVE THEE LIGHT."*

I intend to encourage all readers of this book with the comfort of God's Word.

✝ As things around us continue to change with time,
God remains the same…

✝ *"I am the LORD thy God and I change not…"*
(Malachi 3:6)

✝ His Word shall stand forever (Isaiah 40:8)

God loves you richly and desires the best for you. You are called to be *light* in the midst of darkness. Each of us has important responsibilities at work that transcend our daily tasks. Chances are, they are not listed on our "official" job descriptions.

A CANDLE LOSES NOTHING BY

LIGHTING ANOTHER CANDLE.

"Bear ye one another's burdens,
and so fulfill the law of Christ." (Galatians 6:2)

Student

Athlete

Singer

Executive Assistant

Artist

Laborer

Mechanic

Intern

PART I

The Formative Years...In the Beginning

"And God said, Let there be **light,** *and there was* **light.** *And God saw the light, that it was good: and God divided the light from the darkness."* **(Genesis 1:3-4)**

*T*he formative years represent a period for growth, development and maturation. God is a God of order (1 Corinthians 14:40) and, in the workplace, these three beginning phases are orderly, progressive and build upon each other. Growth, development, and maturation are seasons of new beginnings. When it comes to life experiences, development of character, skills, knowledge, and abilities, and becoming a mature, responsible worker—responsibility breeds accountability and visibility. Also, *"To whom much is given, much is required."* (Luke 12:48)

In the workplace, growth is the phase when we learn to adapt to the environment where God has placed us. The workplace can be compared to a community that functions at its best when people chose to work well together and are genuinely kind to one another. In reality, very few offices function at their best for an extensive period of time due to the sinful nature of man. God's commandment to do unto others, as we would have them to do unto us (Matthew 7:12) is rarely, if ever, actualized. What's desperately needed in the workplace is for God's chosen ones to be the light that will remind your co-workers about the enthusiasm they had when they were first gainfully employed. Remind them of the dreams they had but have lost along the way.

The development of one's skills, abilities, and knowledge is self-initiated as we strive for excellence in our chosen career field. Hard work, practice at what we do, a desire to become the best in our chosen profession, accepting risky assignments, willingness to travel, and moving out of our comfort zone are steps that strengthen our ability and demonstrate a passion to go beyond the call of duty. Be

11

light to others as you develop your skills for a fruitful future in your chosen career field. Exemplify excellence in character, integrity, reliability and workmanship throughout your entire workday. Be the spark that encourages your co-workers to develop their skills and motivate them to follow their dreams.

Maturity is the end result of the growth and development progression. The mature worker accepts responsibility for actions taken and career progression. In the beginning of God's recorded Word, it is written, *"And God said, Let there be light, and there was light. And God saw the light, that it was good: and God divided the light from the darkness."* (Genesis 1:3-4) Light created organization where there once was chaos and it dispelled darkness where it was once void. (Genesis 1:2) This happened in the beginning, before God planted seed that brought forth vegetation (Genesis 1:11). The seeds that we plant into our respective careers will produce fruit in our lives, and equally as important—in the lives of others. Therefore, let your *light* so shine and your maturity illuminate the workplace! Allow your mature approach to office situations and circumstances give others a desire to achieve fruitful results as well.

Chapter One

Growth

"The office is a community, and like other communities, it functions best when people are polite and kind to one another. This means being polite to people at every level of the office hierarchy, not just those who are higher up."

—Complete Book of Etiquette,
Amy Vanderbilt, 1952

"Wherefore laying aside all malice, and all guile, and hypocrisies, and envies, and all evil speakings, as newborn babes, desire the milk of the word, that ye may grow thereby: If so be ye have tasted that the Lord is gracious."
(1 Peter 2:1-3)

Be open to learn and grow.

*I*t is your first day at work. Perhaps, fond memories bring a smile to your face. Maybe not. It's a privilege to be gainfully employed and I view my first day on the job like the day I accepted Jesus Christ as my personal Lord and Saviour. It's a day I choose not to forget. It represents a new beginning. I made a transition from one state to another state—from unemployed to gainfully employed into a secure job. A positive change with a new outlook on life looked back at me when I looked in the mirror.

One year earlier, I had completed my undergraduate studies and desperately wanted to work. At this time in history, The United States was deep into an economic depression under The Reagan Administration. The year was 1983. Finding employment for a recent college graduate with no meaningful work experience can be a daunting task. Finally, my day arrived. Having just celebrated my 24th birthday one week earlier, my first day at work was on July 23, 1984 at The Defense Personnel Support Center in Philadelphia, Pennsylvania. It's still a vivid memory that I cherish. I was passionate and eager to learn and *grow*. I was eager to prove that I belonged and ready to apply what I had learned in college. I liken it to a seed that had just been planted and more than eager to grow up to stand as tall and strong as an oak tree when it is fully mature. I was more than ready to begin what I felt would be a productive career in the field of government contract negotiations and management.

Growth is a key measuring stick for success in the workplace. It is during the growth phase of one's career that the work environment will play a critical role. When it comes to the growth of the worker, it is said, "The elevator to success is out of order. You'll have to use the stairs…one step at a time." In 1 Peter 2:1-3, The Apostle Peter teaches a profound message about growth:

"Wherefore laying aside all malice, and all guile, and hypocrisies, and envies, and all evil speakings, As newborn babes, desire the sincere milk of the word, that ye may **grow thereby***: If so be ye have tasted that the Lord is gracious."*

This is a growth message from one of Jesus' disciples. Persecution can cause either growth or bitterness in the life of Christians. The theme of this book is the proper response to Christian suffering. Peter knew that when the Christians in his audience stood for truth, justice, and fairness, they would need encouraging words to prepare them for the trials that would also come. When you and I stand for truth in the workplace, persecution shall come. Peter writes this letter to give the Jewish believers a divine perspective on such trials so that they will be able and equipped to endure them without wavering in their faith.

> *Some never get started on their destiny because they cannot humble themselves to learn, grow, and change.*

For starters, view your fresh start as a new opportunity to learn, *grow*, and change. Twelve men were selected by Jesus Christ to carry out His mandate—*"To seek and to save that which was lost"* (Luke 19:10)—after His death.

His disciples received instructions, guidance, and counseling, for three and one-half years. A disciple is a student, a follower, a learner and an apprentice. It implies acceptance of the teacher's teachings and imitation of His practices (Luke 6:40 and Isaiah 8:16). Jesus' followers were called disciples (Luke 22:29), as are all Christians (Luke 14:26-27 and Acts 9:36). Part of their growth process was, for some, to abandon their current professions—fishermen (Simon Peter, Andrew, James-son of Zebedee, and John), tax collector

(Matthew), Philip, Bartholomew, Thomas, James (son of Alphaeus), Thaddaeus, Simon (the Zealot), and Judas Iscariot—and follow Jesus. Jesus was their teacher, mentor, advisor, counselor, confidant, and protector. As followers and eyewitnesses, they observed His actions and obeyed His teachings, while taking heed to His consistent nature. Their leader was not a hypocrite, so the followers were open to grow and learn. The Apostle Peter's public message of *growth* is extracted from what he learned from Jesus. During this time in Biblical history, Christians were savagely treated in Rome, and this policy was probably reflected throughout the empire. Also, Christians were found throughout Asia Minor (Republic of Turkey), as stated in chapter one, verse one. Christianity had not yet been received because of the official Roman ban, but the stage was being set for persecution and martyrdom in the near future.

In the book of Romans, The Apostle Paul writes a comforting message designed for the saints at Rome. Paul's writings mirror his gift of exhortation and are overwhelmingly encouraging to his intended audience. During his conversion from King Saul on Damascus Road, he had a conversation with Jesus. Although he was not a disciple of Jesus, Paul bears the title of an apostle because of his personal encounter with Jesus on Damascus Road (Acts 9:4-6). *"For I say, through the grace given unto me, to every man that is among you, not to think of himself more highly than he ought to think; but to think soberly, according as God hath dealt to every man the measure of faith."* (Romans 12:3)

Considered as his greatest work, Paul's message of *growth* focuses on our responsibilities to God. First, we are to recognize that we must offer our bodies a living sacrifice—live a holy lifestyle that is acceptable unto God; eliminate the cursing, bad attitude, backbiting, lying, and whatever does not represent God favorably. That is our reasonable service, or the least that we can do. Next, in carrying out His mandate, we are not to be conformed to this world. Do not follow man's lustful desires for fame, fortune, and prestige. Instead, we are to renew our mind with The Word of God and in accordance to His Will. In doing so, we demonstrate to the world and prove what is good and acceptable. Lastly, we are to think soberly, and not be puffed up, according to the measure of faith that God has dealt to each of us. To be high-minded, means to put one's self before others. That doesn't produce growth, but stagnates it.

Placed first among his thirteen epistles in the New Testament, this book explores the significance of Jesus' sacrificial death. Using a question-and-answer format, Paul records the most systematic presentation of doctrine in *The Holy Bible*. It's a book of practical exhortation—encouragement. Key words such as righteousness, faith, law, all and sin each appear at least sixty times in this book.

THE THREE GROWTH PHASES

Growth is a process that happens over time. It is constant and in most cases, never stops. The workplace is an environment that changes everyday. Our ability, or inability, to be flexible to changes within the workplace can either propel or stifle our personal growth. This process of growth, according to The Word of God, involves two meaningful steps: (1) A correct attitude that is required to promote growth, and humility, as well as the ability to (2) Be ever mindful of the small beginnings. This process is expressly recorded in *The Holy Bible* as a guide for us to follow, apply, and live by. Like the seed that's a small source of life, as it is planted into good ground, it grows into a mature state over time. It reproduces after its own kind. (Genesis 1:11-12)

Grow(th), in the original Greek language, has three meanings:

1. *Auxanō*—"to *grow* or increase," of the growth of that which lives, naturally or spiritually.

2. *Auxēsis*—"increase"—Ephesians 4:16; Colossians. 2:19.

Auxēsis

"From whom the whole body fitly joined together and compacted by that which every joint supplieth, according to the effectual

*working in the measure of every part, maketh **increase** of the
body unto the edifying of itself in love."* (Ephesians 4:16)

God created man in His image and after His likeness (Genesis
1:26). Further, man is fearfully and wonderfully made (Psalm 139:14)
and even the very hairs on our head are all numbered (Matthew
10:30). God designed our body parts to work together in unison so
that we can function at our optimum levels. The more cohesive the
group, the better it works together. Similarly, we are supposed to
grow together as a cohesive group on the job and work without giving
preference to one over another. In which case, God gives the increase.
As God unites Christians with Himself, Christ also brings them into
a harmonious relationship with one another. This harmony is
accomplished *by that which every joint supplieth.* The spiritual gifts
mentioned in verses 7 through 15 are figuratively likened to the
various "joints" or "ligaments" of the body. Christ joins believers
together and unites their divinely-ordained ministries and diverse
spiritual gifts, which are exercised and used among believers for the
common good—even at work. As such, the productivity of everyone
involved increases. And God is glorified as a result.

*"And not holding the Head, from which all the body of joints and
bands having nourishment ministered, and knit together,
increaseth with the **increase** of God."* (Colossians 2:19)

Working together, while acknowledging your role on the team,
is what makes the whole team cohesive, dynamic, and creative. The
Greek word holding means to hold fast to someone as to remain
united with Christ (The Head). *Having nourishment ministered, and
knit* together means being supported and united. From Christ (The
Head), then, the church (the body) derives spiritual growth as it is
supported and untied by the various ministering believers (the joints).
In doing so, we increase in Him and can be the light that is so
desperately needed in the workplace.

3. *Huperauxanō*—"to increase beyond measure", is used of faith and love, in their living and practical effects —2 Thessalonians 1:3.

Huperauxanō

With love as the motivating factor, you cannot fail. Because love never fails.

"We are bound to thank God always for you, brethren, as it is meet, because that your faith groweth exceedingly, and the charity of every one of you all toward each other aboundeth."
(2 Thessalonians 1:3)

The Apostle Paul again expresses his pleasure with the spiritual growth of the intended audience. His earlier fears have been dispelled based upon the testimony of the Thessalonians. This book is Paul's second letter to them in response to certain reports—from Timothy —that had come concerning their progress. What is significant about Paul's message is that he perceived such potential in this "little church to the north" that he established on his second missionary journey. During Paul's day, Thessalonica was the capital of Macedonia. His ministry in the city lasted only one month, yet this city became famous for its wealth as well as its attraction of a strange mixture of Roman high society and pagan sensuality. This influx of cultural diversities created confusion and conflicting beliefs about Jesus Christ. However, this small church's love and faith caused growth beyond measure because it was established upon Paul's steadfast love of Christ.

A CORRECT ATTITUDE TO GROW

Your attitude is one of the few things that is completely under your control. Life is 10% of what happens to us, but 90% of how we respond to life's situations and circumstances. Jesus Christ's first public sermon contains a powerful teaching about the importance of having a correct attitude. He teaches this awesome message after being tempted by Satan on three different occasions. His timing could not have been more crucial. In Matthew, Chapter Four, *The Holy Bible* records the confrontation between Jesus and Satan. Jesus had fasted for forty days and forty nights and was hungry (Verse 2). Satan attempted to persuade Jesus to "partner" with him during this trying time. He mistakenly assumed that Jesus was too weak to resist his three proposals. But, The Word records their conversations as follows:

"If thou be the Son of God, command that these stones be made bread. But He answered and said, It is written, MAN SHALL NOT LIVE BY BREAD ALONE, BUT BY EVERY WORD THAT PROCEEDETH OUT OF THE MOUTH OF GOD. Then the devil taketh Him up into the holy city, and setteth Him on a pinnacle of the temple. And said unto Him, If thou be the Son of God, cast thyself down....Jesus said unto him, It is written again, THOU SHALL NOT TEMPT THE LORD THY GOD. Again, the devil took Him up into an exceeding high mountain, and shewed Him all the kingdoms of this world, and the glory of them; And said unto Him, All these things I will give thee, if thou fall down and worship me. Then Jesus said unto him, Get thee hence, Satan: for it is written, THOU SHALL WORSHIP THE LORD THY GOD, AND HIM ONLY SHALT THOU SERVE."
(Matthew 4:4-10)

"Then the devil leaveth Him, and, behold, angels came and ministered unto Him." (Matthew 4:11)

The Beattitudes—*'The attitude we ought to be'*—is the first message that Jesus delivered in His Sermon on the Mount as recorded in Matthew, Chapter 5, verses 1-12:

"And seeing the multitudes, He went up into a mountain: and when he was set, His disciples came unto Him: And He opened His mouth, and taught them, saying,

:3   Blessed are the poor in spirit: for their's is the kingdom of heaven.

Attitude #1—Humility

> :4   *Blessed are they that mourn, for they shall be comforted.*

Attitude #2 – Concern about the sinful condition of this world.

> :5   *Blessed are the meek: for they shall inherit the earth.*

Attitude #3 – Keep your strength (power) under control.

> :6   *Blessed are they which do hunger and thirst after righteousness: for they shall be filled.*

Attitude #4 – Fulfillment comes from being right with God.

> :7   *Blessed are the merciful: for they shall obtain mercy.*

Attitude #5 – Be compassionate towards the plight of others.

> :8   *Blessed are the pure in heart: for they shall see God.*

Attitude #6 – Be sincere in your actions.

> :9   *Blessed are the peacemakers: for they shall be called the children of God.*

Attitude #7 – Avoid strife, drama, and contentions. Exhibit a peaceful demeanor even in the midst of a storm.

> :10 *Blessed are they which are persecuted for righteousness' sake: for their's is the kingdom of heaven.*

Attitude #8 – Others will not understand that your success is contingent upon your Godly lifestyle and your personal relationship with God, through Jesus Christ. When they resent it and speak evil against you, continue to seek God first and foremost in everything.

> :11 *Blessed are ye, when men shall revile you, and persecute you, and shall say all manner of evil against you falsely, for my sake.*

Attitude #9 – Remain steadfast in the faith. Even Jesus was persecuted.

> :12 *Rejoice, and be exceeding glad: for great is your reward in heaven: for so persecuted they the prophets which were before you."*

A positive attitude is a powerful force. It cannot be stopped.

Do Not Despise The Small Beginnings

Everything big starts with something small. The size of a mustard seed is so small that it is difficult to see. However, when it grows to full maturity, it is one of the largest plants on the face of the earth. Under favorable conditions, its dimensions, after fully mature, can be ten to twelve feet tall after only five months.

"For who hath despised the day of small things? For they shall rejoice, and shall see the plummet of the hand of Zerubbabel with those seven; they are the eyes of the Lord, which run to and fro through the whole earth." (Zechariah 4:10)

One kernel of corn can produce a stalk with two ears, each having 200 kernels. From those 400 kernels come 400 more stalks, which produce 160,000 kernels. and 160,000 more stalks, producing a total of 64 million kernels. The principle of compounding is at work here.[1]

Dr. Polly Matzinger was working as a cocktail waitress when she was "discovered" to be a scientist-in-the-making. Before then, no one would have thought to take her seriously. Today, some think her immune system theory could revolutionize the way we treat disease. For decades, scientists thought the immune system reacts to foreign cells entering the body. Instead, Dr. Matzinger postulates that the system responds only when it receives signals from injured cells. "Think of the body as a community that welcomes visitors," she says, "but alerts the cops when someone starts breaking windows. In the same way, the immune system is alerted by damage-induced alarm signals, not foreign cells." Dr. Matzinger's Danger Model challenges the theory on how the body defends itself. Now section head of The National Institute of Allergy and Infectious Diseases in Bethesda, Maryland, Dr. Matzinger began in an unrelated field of endeavor. This college dropout, dog trainer, jazz musician, carpenter, and waitress, found each of her jobs boring. It was through conversations with faculty members who frequented the bar that she

---

[1] ***Word for Today***—Bob Gass, April 30, 2002

interjected her knowledge about evolutionary adaptations in skunks and earned the attention of the faculty. She was then encouraged to become a scientist and completed her field of study by earning a Ph.D. from the University of California at San Diego. "What's nice about science is if things don't make sense, you can question them and not get fired for it."[2]

"You don't have much experience, but I'm impressed by how you've blown it out of proportion."

©2003; Reprinted courtesy of Bunny Hoest and Parade.

...walk worthy in the job that you have

"I therefore, the prisoner of the Lord, beseech you that ye walk worthy of the vocation wherewith ye are called." (Ephesians 4:1)

Your walk should reflect your calling. Bring credit to His name everyday. God doesn't call the qualified, He qualifies the called. Live in a manner befitting the divine call that summoned you to salvation.

BASIC WORKPLACE MANNERS

At 50, *Complete Book of Etiquette* covers traditional social mores and lifestyle advice. Here are some guidelines for manners in the workplace from Amy Vanderbilt's book:

---

[2] *Parade Magazine*, by Michael Ryan, "She's Not Afraid to Ask Questions," March 24, 2002.

ON THE JOB	"The office is a community, and like other communities, it functions best when people are polite and kind to one another. This means being polite to people at every level of the office hierarchy, not just those who are higher up."
ON THE INTERVIEW	"Take note: People have sometimes been offered jobs because they were the only applicant to write a thank-you letter to the person who conducted the interview. This simple, courteous gesture demonstrates these three valuable qualities…motivation, enthusiasm and responsibility."
ON INTRODUCTIONS	"Sometimes you may be greeted by someone whose name you have forgotten and have to introduce him to a third person. It's tempting to avoid or postpone the introduction while you feverishly search your mind for the name. Instead, simply say, I'm sorry, but your name suddenly escapes me."
ON FIRING SOMEONE	"Always deliver the news in private —either in your office or in the employee's. The latter may be more appropriate as, when you leave, employee is free to shut the door, cry, get angry, or call his spouse."

ON BEING FIRED	"It's only natural to feel upset, but if you panic or react in anger, it won't help the situation. You need to behave in a way that will increase the likelihood of finding a new position as quickly as possible."[3]

Recognizing and acknowledging the three phases of growth, having a proper attitude aligned with the will of God, excelling in your role, and having basic workplace manners, will assist you to develop the foundational skills necessary to successfully compete on the job. Seek first the Kingdom, and His righteousness, and God will provide you with the 'things' that you need to sustain you. —(Matthew 6:33)

---

[3] First published in 1952, *Complete Book of Etiquette*, the 50th anniversary edition is newly released. *Sunday Star Ledger* newspaper, Accent Section, March 17, 2002, by Kathleen O'Brien, staff writer.

FOOD FOR THOUGHT ON GROWTH

GOD'S PHOTO ALBUM

In a book entitled ***God's Photo Album*** by Shelly Mecum and the children and families of Our Lady of Perpetual Help School, rests an inspirational story about how they looked for God and saved their school. Ms. Mecum and her students had a dream, and the courage & faith, to make their dream soar. Determined to save the struggling Ewa Beach Elementary School on Oahu, Hawaii, they mobilized an entire community to realize her vision: a spiritual quest for God and a brave book-writing adventure. Some 168 young children and their families, ranging from five to eighty years old, toted cameras, notebooks, and pencils across the island by bus, trolley, and glass-bottom boat. Their mission? To find ***God***. Enclosed throughout the pages of this wonderful book are snapshots and inspiring observations, offering unforgettable moments of grace. Proof that no dream is too big!

Chapter Two

Development

"I've missed more than 9,000 shots in my career,
I've lost almost 300 games,
26 times, I've been trusted to take the game winning shot,
and missed. I've FAILED over and over and over again in my life. And that is why I SUCCEED."
—Michael Jordan, 1997 Nike Ad reflecting on the career of the world's greatest professional basketball player.

"The entrance of thy words giveth **light;** *it giveth under-standing unto the simple."* (Psalm 119:130)

Develop skills along the way. Never stop learning.

*F*ew would argue that the best basketball player ever in the National Basketball Association (NBA) is Michael Jordan. His career statistics, prior to his second and third retirement from the game, speak for themselves:

2	Olympic gold medals (1984 and 1992)
3	NBA All-Star Game Most Valuable Player (1988, 1996, 1998)
5	NBA regular season MVPs (1988, 1991, 1992, 1996, 1998)
6	NBA Finals MVPs (NBA record)
9	NBA All-Defensive First Team selections (NBA record)
10	NBA scoring titles (NBA record)
21.3	All-Star scoring average (NBA record)
26	Free throws made in 27 attempts versus the New Jersey Nets on February 26, 1987
31.5	Regular season scoring average
33.4	Playoff scoring average (NBA record)
35	Points scored in first half of 1992 NBA Finals Game 1 (NBA record)
41	Scoring average, 1993 NBA Finals versus the Phoenix Suns (NBA Finals record)
63	Points scored versus the Boston Celtics on April 20, 1986 (NBA Playoff record)
69	Points scored versus the Cleveland Cavaliers on March 28, 1990 (career high)
5,987	Playoff points scored (NBA record)
29,277	Regular season point scored[4]

---

[4] ***Upper Deck Collectibles***, 1999. Authenticated number 10,126 of 99,000 printed.

However, the initial rejection and an inability to earn a roster spot on the high school varsity basketball team was the spark that lit the fire! The heart of this champion was revealed publicly, in April 1982, during the Division I College Basketball National Championship game in New Orleans, Louisiana—Georgetown University versus The University of North Carolina. As a college freshman, Jordan helped his team win the game by having the courage to launch a fifteen-foot jump shot with only a few remaining seconds left in the regulation game. His team trailed by one point. As the ball left his hand, the capacity crowd of 15,000+ cheering fans echoed the infamous chant, WHOOOSH! which was symbolic of knowing that the ball is going into the basket. At that point, Carolina led by one point. An unforced turnover by a Georgetown University guard sealed Carolina's victory.

At the professional level, Michael developed his game throughout his career and ultimately led a struggling franchise in the city of Chicago to six NBA championships. This franchise defeated a different team each time. It began in the 1990-1991 season against the high flying Los Angeles Lakers and their star Magic Johnson. It ended in the 1997-1998 season against the fundamentally sound and precision-like Utah Jazz and their stars John Stockton and Karl Malone.

Probably the closest to perfection a person ever comes is when he or she fills out a job application form.[5]

We are all faced with a series of great opportunities brilliantly disguised as impossible situations. In times of change, learners inherit the earth while the learned find they are beautifully equipped to deal with a world that no longer exists.

Development (a noun) is defined as the act or process of developing. It also means *maturity*—a developed state or form. Develop (a verb) is defined as follows: (1) To bring out the possibilities of; Bring to a more advanced, effective, or usable state; (2) To cause to grow or expand; (3) To bring into being or activity;

---

[5] Stanley J. Randall

produce; (4) To cause to mature or evolve; (5) To grow into a mature state; advance; expand.

CONNECT TO GOD

Your Mind

'Mind' is used 95 times in *The Holy Bible*. In the original Greek form—*nous*—it means the seat of reflective consciousness, comprising the faculties of perception and understanding, and those of feeling, judging and determining. The mind is the divine center of choice. Choices are long-lasting and life-changing. It is also where our thoughts reside. Thoughts become words, words become actions, actions become habits. Our habits shape our character, and our character will determine our future.[6]

In the November 6, 2000 issue of *U.S. News and World Report*, entitled "How to Master the New Workplace, Career Guide 2001," the opening statement under the subtitle on page 56 is self-explanatory: *The new workplace is risky, rugged, and rewarding. And guess what? You're in charge!* The Apostle Paul, in his letter to the Romans, emphasizes upon that point. Our environment at work is risky, rugged, and rewarding, and we are in charge. Paul writes: *"...be ye not conformed to this world: but be ye transformed by the renewing of your **mind**, that ye may prove what is that good, and acceptable, and perfect will of God."* (Romans 12:2) We are to resist being poured into the mold of the present thinking, value systems, and conduct of this world. 'Be not conformed' is only used again in 1 Peter 1:14.

With our minds, we can understand God's word, if we choose to do so. Understanding God's Word requires readiness and an act of our will (*attitude*). There are two words in the original Greek language that best describe using our minds to understand:

Ginōskō—to allow oneself to learn, and
Manthanō—to understand learning.

---

[6] ***Success Guide***, by Shane Idleman, Issue 101, January 2001

Used together, they have a tri-fold meaning:

- to allow oneself to increase in knowledge,
- to learn by use and practice, and
- to allow understanding by an act of one's will.

"The entrance of thy words giveth light; it giveth understanding unto the simple." (Psalm 119:130)

Your Body

The principle of isometrics is that you can build muscle by pushing firmly against an unyielding object. You can build character the same way. —Phyllis Haxton

This principle applies to the human body as well. 'Body' is referenced 173 times in *The Holy Bible*. In the original Greek—*soma*—means the body as a whole, the instrument of life, whether of man living (Matthew 6:22), or dead (Matthew 27:52). 'Vessel,' has various meanings in the context of the English language. Specifically, as it relates to the human body, it is defined as a person regarded as a holder or receiver of a particular trait or quality. In the original Greek, *skeuos*, it means "for the service of God" (Acts 9:15), "a chosen vessel" (2 Timothy 2:21), "an earthen vessel" (2 Corinthians 4:7), "the human frame" (2 Corinthians 4:7 and 1 Thessalonians 4:4), and "the subjects of divine mercy and wrath" (Romans 9:22-23). It is used 193 times in *The Holy Bible* in both its singular and plural forms. We are vessels, used by God to carry out His will in the earth and on our respective jobs. For reasons He never explains, He chooses to work through ordinary people like us. He placed us in situations that ultimately unlock our compassion and creativity. He connects us with people who can open doors that we cannot open because of a lack of proper equipment or knowledge. Wherever we go, He makes a solution for us. Forming a vessel is a lifelong process. If the potter does not continually wet the clay, it becomes too hard and is unable to be worked. Therefore, allow God to 'shape' you into the vessel He desires so that He can use you mightily!

"And the vessel that he made of clay was marred in the hand of the potter: so he made it again another vessel, as seemed good to the potter to make it." (Jeremiah 18:4)

We were bought with a price. Our "bodies" do not belong to us. The Scriptures says, *"The EARTH is the LORD'S, and the fullness thereof, the world, and they that dwell therein."* (Psalm 24:1) Since we belong to Him, we are to use our bodies for His service. This is why the Lord repeatedly teaches us to flee from sexual sins. Sin requires us to use the body in a manner unfitting for Kingdom use. *"What? Know ye not that your body is the temple of the Holy Ghost which is in you, which ye have of God, and ye are not your own? For ye are bought with a price: therefore glorify God in your body, and in your spirit, which are God's."* (1 Corinthians 6:19-20)

The price paid was the blood of Jesus Christ (Acts 20:28). This has profound significance for the believer (1 Timothy 4:10 and 1 Peter 2:9) who has been called out of darkness into His marvelous light.

Develop Into Your Role

I am, just as you are, a unique, never-to-be-repeated event in this universe. Therefore, I have, just as you have, a unique, never-to-be-repeated role in this world —George Sheehan

Before you set goals, discover your God-ordained purpose. You have the ministry (*of reconciliation*) whether you know it or not. People are dying because they don't know what Jesus has done for them. The economy is no longer robust, as it was under the Clinton Administration. Corporate executives are being openly punished and humiliated, as they should, for willful misconduct that negatively affects the lives of thousands of employees. Multi-billion dollar corporations are filing for bankruptcy protection as a means to save face while, at the same time, personal bankruptcy is at an all time high. Police officers are still being videotaped abusing their authority as witnessed in Englewood, California in the summer of 2002. The value of family has deteriorated to the extent of becoming less meaningful than one's desire to please their employer. The dot-com and telecommunications bubbles that once seemed impenetrable have burst. Many developing countries are wastelands of poverty, hunger, and disease. But, as faithful believers in Christ, we have the answer. Look at some of His benefits and provisions that He has for His chosen children:

"Let your conversation be without covetousness; and be content with such things as ye have: for he hath said, I will never leave thee, nor forsake thee." (Hebrews 13:5)

Benefit/Provision # 1—God's provisions are eternal.

"Behold, I give you power to tread on serpents and scorpions, and over all the power of the enemy: and nothing shall by any means hurt you." (Luke 10:19)

Benefit/Provision # 2—We have authority over spiritual wickedness in high places in the name of Jesus.

"The thief cometh not, but for to steal, and to kill, and to destroy: I am come that they might have life, and that they might have it more abundantly." (John 10:10)

Benefit/Provision # 3—We are no longer subject to the power of darkness but have been translated into the marvelous light! Satan no longer has authority over our lives.

"Thou wilt keep him in perfect peace, whose mind is stayed on thee: because he trusteth in thee." (Isaiah 26:3)

Benefit/Provision # 4—Peace will keep you healthy and functional within The Kingdom of God.

There are so many awesome benefits and provisions in *The Holy Bible* that The Lord has provided for us. To know them, however, we must become intimately acquainted with Him and His holy

Word. Otherwise, you could finish up somewhere you should not be or succeed at something God never called you to do.

Benefit/Provision # 5—To lose is not always failure.

"This poor man cried, and the LORD heard him, and saved him out of all his troubles." (Psalm 37:6)

Benefit/Provision #6—Knowing about God is fascinating; Knowing God personally is life changing.

"But let him that glorieth glory in this, that he understandeth and knoweth me, that I am the LORD which exercise lovingkindness, judgment, and righteousness, in the earth: for in these things I delight, saith the LORD." (Jeremiah 9:24)

Benefit/Provision # 7—There are legions of angels helping us, for which the world has no counter-measures.

"The angel of the LORD encampeth round about them that fear Him, and delivereth them." (Psalm 34:7)

Benefit/Provision # 8—Faith sees things that are out of sight.

"Are they not all ministering spirits, sent forth to minister for them who shall be heirs of salvation?" (Hebrews 1:14)

ALLOW GOD TO USE YOU

There is no past too troubled and no person that God cannot redeem. He took a murderer name Moses and made him a prophet. He took a liar and cheat named Jacob, made him a prince named Israel and blessed his seed. He took a prostitute named Rahab, called her blessed and changed her profession. He took a Christian hater named Saul and made him a great apostle—Paul. Skilled workers are always in demand and admired.

"Seeth thou a man diligent in his business? He shall stand before kings; he shall not stand before mean men." (Proverbs 22:29)

Every step counts. You are headed in the right direction when you walk with God. It's important to stay spiritually fit by walking with God, which *The Holy Bible* describes as an intimate, growing relationship with the Lord. Enoch walked with God three hundred years (Genesis 5:22). Noah was a just man, perfect in his generations. Noah walked with God (Genesis 6:9). Both men are mentioned in the Book of Hebrews, chapter 11, where they are commended for their faith. Enoch, in verse 5, was translated that he should not see death. Noah, in verse 7, was moved with fear and built an ark to the saving of his household. By doing so, he condemned the world and became heir of the righteousness by faith. The work Jesus accomplished for us, the Holy Spirit now enacts. The spirit searches all things. God, Our Heavenly Father, always communicates with our spirit.

"But as it is written, EYE HATH NOT SEEN, NOR EAR HEARD,
NEITHER HAVE ENTERED INTO THE HEART OF MAN, THE
THINGS WHICH GOD HATH PREPARED FOR THEM THAT LOVE
HIM. But God hath revealed them unto us by His Spirit; for the
Spirit searcheth all things, yea, the deep things of God."
(1 Corinthians 2:9-10)

ALL AUTHORITY IS ORDAINED OF GOD

Stay under authority. It is God's plan to protect your life. The higher powers are established by God as expressly stated in Titus 3:1, 1 Peter 2:13, and Acts 5:29. As parents protect and nurture their sons and daughters, God protects His children. As a boss protects and encourages their staff, God protects His children. As a pastor protects and prays for their congregation, God protects His children. It is ordained by God that we respect and obey those in leadership. Staying under authority serves as protection, even though, at the time, we may not "see" its benefits. Respecting authority is a spiritual law.

"Let every soul be subject unto the higher powers. For there is no
power but of God: the powers that be are ordained of God."
(Romans 13:1)

The higher powers are established by God. Respect and obey the authority that has been placed over you, for that is your protection.

"I should never have asked to speak to her supervisor."

©2003; Reprinted courtesy of Bunny Hoest and Parade.

"Put them in mind to be subject to principalities and powers, to obey magistrates, to be ready to every good work." (Titus 3:1)

Christian citizenship requires us to be subject to those in positions of authority. Obey their instruction and stay ready to work.

"Submit yourselves to every ordinance of man for the Lord's sake: whether it be to the king, as supreme; Or unto governors, as unto them that are sent by him for punishment of evildoings, and for the praise of them that do well." (1 Peter 2:13-14)

Be obedient to natural laws, for The Lord's sake, as well as spiritual laws.

"...We ought to obey God rather than men." (Acts 5:29)

Seek to please and obey Our Heavenly Father first and foremost in your life.

GET PREPARED

Like it or not, all workers are facing a workplace future that will include changing jobs and changing careers. Even in the fast and fluid 2001 economy, workers were losing, finding, abandoning, and embracing jobs at fast-forward speed. A recent U.S. Census Bureau survey reports the difference in lifetime earnings for the holder of a high school diploma and a bachelor's degree is about one million dollars. Those with professional degrees earn much more—about 4.4 million dollars during their working life. It's never too late to go back to school or to sharpen your skills about the trends in the job market. Many adults, and young people as well, have revamped or redirected their careers mid-stream and earned new or additional degrees. With advances in technology, you can now earn your degree online, from an accredited college or university in your spare time, from the comfort of your own home. The following are helpful online resources that will guide you to carefully plan your career progression:

A Web Tutorial

Most accredited colleges and universities offer on-line degree programs in a variety of career fields. These institutions of higher learning have websites that list all of their services, including the on-line course offerings and schedules. To learn more about these courses, visit their website.

Prepping for a job interview:
- www.hoovers.com—Thousands of company capsules outline financial data, list key competitors, and link to related news articles.
- www.newslink.org—Find out what's being said about a company in its hometown with these links to newspapers across the country. For example, the volume of job openings posted on one company website worried a job seeker. Was the company growing or having trouble retaining staff? A search of the local paper's site turned up articles dishing on the company's reputation as a hard place to work.
- www.work.com—A search turns up a company's press releases.

Show you've done your homework by referencing their latest marketing information.
By: Sage Dillon

Show yourself the money:
- www.salary.com—The broadest salary-compensation site. Its Salary Wizard allows you to pick a job category and a region and to quickly find median salaries by position. There's also news on compensation and benefit trends.
- www.wageweb.com—Designed for human-resource professionals, who pay $169 to $219 annually for detailed salary data, the site lets others surf salaries on a national basis for free. Information is current, drawn from surveys of its members, making it a good benchmarking tool.
- www.nationjob.com—This database for job seekers allows you to search by salary level.
- www.bls.gov/ocohome.htm—At this Department of Labor site, you can determine which jobs have good growth prospects and median annual salaries.
- www.4.webpoint.com/townnews_job/reloc_calc3.htm—Seeking a quieter life but afraid you can't match your existing salary in your hometown? With this calculator, select the city you live in, the city you'd like to move to, and your salary to see how many bucks you'll need for the same bang.
  By: Tim Smart

Other key information:
- www.pcepd.gov
- 800-526-7234—The Job Accommodation Network advises employers and employees about workplace accommodations.
- www.eeoc.gov—Equal Employment Opportunity Commission
- www.usdoj.gov—Department of Justice

END YOUR DAY WITH A WORD OF PRAYER

Before you turn out the light, turn to The Light of God's Word.

FOOD FOR THOUGHT ON DEVELOPMENT

ACRES OF DIAMONDS—PART I

In 1870, Journalist Russell Conwell was traveling in what was then Mesopotamia, when he heard the tale of a prosperous Persian farmer, Ali Hafed. Lured by stories of fabulous hidden wealth, he deserted his fruitful farm in search of a mythical diamond field. Far and wide he roamed, but he never found his dream. Eventually, he died a disillusioned pauper. Not long afterwards, acres of diamonds were found on Ali Hafed's land.

Conwell discovered a great truth in this story: Your diamonds are not in far-away mountains or distant seas. They are in your own backyard if you will dig for them. Although he went on to author 40 books and was a famous orator, Conwell is most remembered for his lecture entitled, "Acres of Diamonds," that he delivered more than 6,000 times in towns across America.[7]

[7]*The One Minute Millionaire* by Mark Victor Hansen and Robert G. Allen—Daily Millionaire Minutes ©2002.

Chapter Three

Maturity

"In all human affairs there are things both certain and doubtful, and both are equally in the hands of God, who is accustomed to guide to a good end the causes that are just and are sought with diligence."
—Isabella of Spain, 1451-1504

"For promotion cometh neither from the east, nor from the west, nor from the south. But God is the judge: He putteth down one, and setteth up another." **(Psalm 75:6-7)**

**Responsibility and Accountability
are measures of Maturity.**

*E*xcellence never happens by accident. We have to make it happen. Our methods matter every bit as much as our results. Excellence requires a process. It is not just an outcome.

Maturity is a direct result of excellence. How we react to the situations, people, and circumstances on the job is manifested through our maturity. Maturity, as used in *The Holy Bible*, also means "perfected." In the Greek—*teleios*—it has two meanings: "Having reached its end," and "finished, complete, perfect." Used primarily to refer to persons' physical development, maturity also brings out ethical importance. In this sense, maturity denotes "fully grown" or of full age (1 Corinthians 2:6; 14:20, Ephesians 4:13, Philippians 3:15, Colossians 1:28, 4:12, and Hebrews 5:14).

1 Corinthians 2:6—*"Howbeit we speak wisdom among them that are perfect: yet not the wisdom of this world, nor of the princes of this world, that come to nought?"*

'Perfect' refers to the morally and spiritually *mature*.

1 Corinthians 14:20—*"Brethren, be not children in understanding: howbeit in malice be ye children, but in understanding be men."*

Greek word	Meaning	Three-fold meaning when used together
Ginoskō	To allow oneself to learn	(1) To allow oneself to increase in knowledge; (2) To learn by use and practice, and
Manthanō	To understand learning	(3) To allow understanding by an act of one's will.

Ephesians 4:13—*"Until we all come in the unity of the faith, and of the knowledge of the Son of God, unto a perfect man, unto the measure of the stature of the fullness of Christ."*

Maturity requires us to continually seek after the knowledge of God.

Philippians 3:15—*"Let us therefore as many as be perfect, be thus minded: and if any thing ye be otherwise minded, God shall reveal even this unto you."*

'Perfect', or mature, requires us to have the mind of Christ and to be serious about the Great Commandment of God—*"Go ye therefore, and teach all nations, baptizing them in the name of the Father, and of the Son, and of the Holy Ghost: Teaching them to observe all things whatsoever I have commanded you: and, lo, I am with you always, even unto the end of the world."* (Matthew 28:19-20)

Colossians 1:28 – *"Whom ye preach, warning every man, and teaching every man in all wisdom; that we may present every man perfect in Christ Jesus."*

Consistently and persistently spread the good news of Jesus Christ. Have a desire in your heart to let everyone know that Jesus is Lord!

Colossians 4:12—*"Epaphras, who is one of you, a servant of Christ, saluteth you, always labouring fervently for you in prayers, that ye may stand perfect and complete in all the will of God."*

You may appear perfect and fully assured in all His will. It means literally to the Colossians—being ushered into God's heavenly presence in a morally perfect state.

Hebrews 5:14—*"But strong meat belongeth to them that are of full age, even those who by reason of use have their senses exercised to discern both good and evil."*

To be mature means to be complete, finished and grown up in the things of God. No more struggles with the basic principles of Christianity, but having moved on to become mature representatives of Christ in this earth. Mature Christians must let their light shine at all times—On their jobs—during team meetings, before customers, during strategy sessions—and while training others for their jobs. In good times as well as during troubled times.

> *Blessed is the man who finds out which way God is moving and then gets going in the same direction.*

CHANGE WILL CAUSE MATURITY

Change is life giving. It helps us grow into someone greater than we are already. If you're not riding the wave of change, you'll find yourself beneath it. Sometimes within the waves of change, we find our true direction.

In this rapidly-changing society, we find ourselves in a constant state of transition. What currently works, becomes outdated in a hurry. Three key factors drive change in life and in the workplace—people, technology and information.

People create change. Scientific evidence reveals that human creations have been around for some six or seven million years. It took that long for the population of the earth to reach 5.3 billion people. Predictions say it will take only about fifty years for the next 5.3 billion people to inhabit the earth. If people bring about change —and we do—then we can naturally expect a rapid increase in the rate of change as the population doubles in the next few decades.

Technology, too, leads to change. Evidence will prove that approximately 80% of our technological inventions have occurred since 1900. It was predicted that within the last 15 years of the twentieth century, we would see as much technological change as there had been in the first 85 years of the century. Today, technology is literally multiplying daily.

Information and *knowledge* are power! There was more information produced between 1965 and 1995 (30-years) than was produced in the preceding 5,000-year period from 3,000 B.C. to 1965. Information available in the world is doubling every five years and is becoming available to many more people than it ever reached before. There is far more knowledge, reaching more people, faster than ever before. A better-informed population means better chances for change.

Change has no conscience. It does not play favorites and takes no prisoners. Unfortunately, it does ruthlessly destroy organizations with cultures that do not adapt. Observe what has happened to multiple companies over the past five years and the devastating impact on their employees. A world of high-speed change calls for radical shifts in behavior and a steadfast reliance upon The One who does not change—God Almighty.

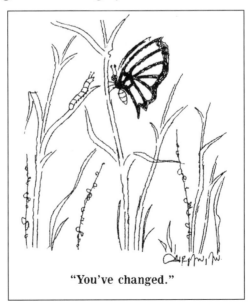

"You've changed."

From *The Wall Street Journal*—Permission, Cartoon Features Syndicate.

MATURITY IN THE WORKPLACE

A View of the Federal Government Workplace

Our goal is to make the entire federal government both less expensive and more efficient, and to change the culture of our national bureaucracy away from complacency and entitlement toward initiative and empowerment. We intend to redesign, to reinvent, and reinvigorate the entire national government.
      —President Bill Clinton, Remarks announcing the National Performance Review March 3, 1993

In 1993, The Clinton Administration took on a bold and daunting task—to reform the federal government. It was called *The National Performance Review*. It is about making changes—historic changes —in the way the government works. Its four-fold mission is as follows: Cutting Red Tape (the bureaucracy), Putting Customers First (service is key), Empowering Employees to Get Results (valuing the human resources for the assets they are), and Cutting Back to Basics (taking common sense to higher places). I am proud to have participated in this dynamic project for six years, from 1993 to 1999, in the area of procurement reform. Through assignments at the Office of Federal Procurement Policy (OFPP) in Washington, DC, I was called upon to give testimony before the United States House of Representatives Committee on Small Business, and presentations before the National Contract Management World Congress, on three occasions. They were hallmark events of my government career.

The core of *The National Performance Review* is expressed in unison by President Clinton and Vice President Gore:

We can no longer afford to pay more for—and get less from—our government. The answer for every problem cannot always be another program or more money. It is time to radically change the way government operates—to shift from top-down bureaucracy to entrepreneurial government that empowers citizens and communities to change our country from the bottom up.

We must reward the people and ideas that work and get rid of those that don't.

Reduce paperwork?

A Government that works better and costs less requires efficient and effective information systems. The Paperwork Reduction Act of 1995 and the Information Technology Management Reform Act of 1996 provide the opportunity to improve significantly the way the Federal Government acquires and manages information technology. Agencies now have the clear authority and responsibility to make measurable improvements in mission performance and service delivery to the public through the strategic application of information technology. A coordinated approach that builds on existing structures and successful practices is needed to provide maximum benefit across The Federal Government from this technology. Accordingly, by the authority vested in me as President by the Constitution and the laws of the United States of America, it is hereby ordered as follows...

—Opening paragraphs of Executive Order
    13011, Federal Information Technology,
    July 16, 1996, William Jefferson Clinton,
    President of the United States

The eleven sections in this Executive Order define the policies and procedures that will govern the strategic shift of the federal government into the information age. Section One states, in part, that the policy of the United States Government is that executive agencies shall:

(a) significantly improve the management of their information systems, including the acquisition of information technology;

(b) refocus information technology management to support directly their strategic missions;

(c) establish clear accountability for information resources management activities by creating agency Chief Information Officers (CIO's) with the visibility and management responsibilities necessary to advise the agency head on the design, development, and implementation of those information systems.

(d) cooperate in the use of information technology to improve the productivity of Federal programs and to promote a coordinated, interoperable, secure, and shared Government-wide infrastructure that is provided and supported by a diversity of private sector suppliers and a well-trained corps of information technology professionals;

(e) establish an interagency support structure that builds on existing successful interagency efforts.

Employee's Views

Adherence to the Merit Principles in the Workplace, Federal Employees' Views is a federal government study of the workplace environment. This report was compiled and issued by the U.S. Merit Systems Protection Board, Office of Policy and Evaluation, as a report to the President and Congress of the United States. The report summarizes the responses from 9,710 Federal employees, in 1997, who were asked to assess the extent to which their respective agencies take actions that are consistent with the merit principles. Its goal is to obtain the views of Federal employees on a number of workplace issues such as working conditions, job satisfaction, and the quality of coworkers and supervisors. The merit system principles embody a set of values that lie at the heart of public service, and their purpose is to ensure that the trust the public has placed in the Federal Government to operate a personnel system based on merit is earned.

The Merit System Principles, which were articulated in statute in the 1978 Civil Service Reform Act, are a set of values for Federal public service that date back to the beginning of the merit-based civil service system in 1883. The principles address basic human resource management activities. These activities—including selections, promotions, and actions to deal with performance problems—define the goals that all Federal managers are expected to strive for when managing their workforce. They are meant to ensure that Government processes and systems for selecting and maintaining the Federal workforce will result in a competent workforce that serves the best interests of the American people. These questions were asked of employees of every grade plus the Senior Executive Service as part of the 1996 Merit Principles Survey, a Government-wide survey that MSPB has conducted approximately every three years since 1983 to assess the health of the merit system. These results are from the 20th anniversary of the 1978 Civil Service Reform Act. Substantial minorities of respondents believed violations were occurring that undermine the merit system. The findings of this fifth survey since 1983 are mixed:

- According to employees, budget cuts, downsizing, and reinvention efforts have had noticeable effects, both positive and negative, on the operation of many Federal organizations.
- Efforts to reinvent the way the Government does business have not been pursued to the same degree by all agencies.
- Results of reinvention efforts are mixed overall.
- Employees have a positive view of their jobs and organizations.
- Problem employees remain a significant problem for many Federal supervisors.
- Employees continue to be concerned about prohibited personnel practices.

Based upon the key findings and results of the 1996 Merit Principles Survey, the following recommendations were made:

- Agencies and organizations should make sure that their efforts to reduce expenditures also include a sincere effort to involve employees in attempts to improve operations.

- In many Federal organizations there is a culture that sanctions not dealing effectively with problem employees. This must be changed for the Government to be able to hold employees accountable for their performance.

- Efforts should be made by the Office of Personnel Management and individual agencies to ensure that the Government maintains its ability to find and recruit high-quality applicants.

- In a time of greater decentralization and delegation of personnel management authorities, it is increasingly important to ensure that an effective and visible system is in place to ensure that supervisors are held accountable for the decisions they make.

A View of the Corporate Workplace

*"The quest for excellence into the twenty-first century begins in the schoolroom, but we must go next to the **workplace**. More than 20 million new jobs will be created before the new century unfolds and by then, our economy should be able to provide a job for everyone who wants to work. We must enable our workers to adapt to the rapidly changing nature of the workplace..."*

—President Ronald Reagan
State of the Union Address
January 27, 1987

In an executive summary prepared by The Hudson Institute of Indianapolis, Indiana entitled, *"Workforce 2000—Work and Workers for the 21st Century,"* June 1987, it was predicted that four trends would shape the last years of the twentieth century:

• The American economy should grow at a relatively healthy pace.

• Despite its international comeback, U.S. manufacturing will be a much smaller share of the economy in the year 2000.

• The workforce will grow slowly, becoming older, more female, and more disadvantaged. Only 15 percent of the new entrants to the labor force over the next 13 years will be native white males, compared to 47 percent in that category in 1987.

• The new jobs in service industries will demand much higher skill levels than the jobs in the middle 1980's.

The executive summary left us with sis challenges:
- Stimulating Balanced World Growth
- Accelerating Productivity Increases in Service Industries
- Maintaining the Dynamism of an Aging Workforce
- Reconciling the Conflicting Needs of Women Who Work
- Considering Their Families and
- Integrating Black and Hispanic Workers Fully into the Economy

Unfortunately, instead of responding to President Reagan's challenge to enable our workers to adapt to the rapidly-changing nature of the workplace, the corporate workplace has become mired in its own love for money, greed, speed to market, and latest management fads that have failed its citizens. Conversely, as the day-to-day focus on profits and speed deflect the good intentions of the *Workforce 2000* report, the six challenges have only gained minimal momentum.

In June 2002, President George W. Bush outlined a ten-point plan designed to improve corporate responsibility and help protect America's shareholders. These proposals are guided by the following core principles: 1) providing better information to investors; 2) making corporate officers more accountable; and 3) developing a stronger, more independent audit system. Proposals one and two come under the sub-heading—**Better Information for Investors.** Proposals three through six come under the sub-heading—**Making Corporate Officers Accountable.** Proposals seven through ten come under the sub-heading **Developing a Strong, More Independent Audit System.** In an excerpt from a June 28, 2002 speech on corporate responsibility, Mr. Bush said, "We expect high standards in our schools, we expect high standards in corporate offices as well. And I intend to enforce the law to make sure that there are high standards." (Applause)[8]

---

[8] For more information on the President's Ten-Point Plan, see http:// www.whitehouse.gov.news/releases/2002/03/20020307.html)

Understanding Diversity

Cultural diversity has become an essential part of the workplace within the past ten years. Countless numbers of dollars, energy, and resources have been expended on attempts—some successful, some wasteful—to "level the playing field" and promote "fair access" to all who desire an equal opportunity to compete for jobs. In an article entitled, *"Has 'Minority' Become a Dirty Word?"* by Yoji Cole, the author best summarizes why man's solution to a God-ordained calling will not and cannot work for the benefit of all who are involved:

> *"The politically correct speakers in the nation have gone from using 'Negro' to 'Black' to 'African American'; from using 'Spanish' to 'Hispanic' to 'Latino;' from using 'Oriental' to 'Asian' to 'Asian American.' Then, of course, there is the all-encompassing word 'minority.' 'Minority,' however, is falling out of favor with a growing number of people throughout the country. People who would rather see the word disappear from the Colonial English dictionary say the word has become a stamp for those who lack proper education, economic opportunity, that lacked drive, initiative, and a pursuit of excellence. In effect, 'minority,' has become the stereotype. 'When people are afraid to speak about issues of race because they might use the wrong word and then get slammed, they stop talking,' says Howard Ross, President of diversity consultants Cook Ross, Inc. 'The most important thing that people can, and should do, if we are going to move forward regarding these issues, is to be talking.'"* [9]

Today's workforce includes more women—increasingly in high-paying professions such as law—but far fewer seniors and farmers:

---

[9] Diversity Inc.com, February 11, 2002

A View of the workplace in general terms

Working Category	1900	2000[10]
Married Women in Labor Force	8%	61% (1998)
Single Women in Labor Force	44%	69% (1998)
Men Over 65 in Labor Force	63%	17% (1998)
Female Lawyers	1%	29% (1998)
Factory Workers' Hourly Wage (inflation adjusted)	$3.80 (1909)	$13.90 (1999)
Union Members (share of civilian labor force)	3%	12% (1998)
Family Farms	5.7 million	1.9 million (1997)
War Veterans	1.1 million	25.1 million (1998)

PROMOTION COMES FROM GOD

"For promotion cometh neither from the east, nor from the west, nor from the south. But God is the judge: he putteth down one, and setteth up another." (Psalm 75:6-7)

---

[10]*U.S. News and World Report,* Cover Story—"Who We Were, Who We Are America 1900-2000: How an Epic Century Changed a Nation", August 6, 2001, page 18 and *The First Measured Century*, U.S. Census Bureau, *Statistical Abstract of the United States.*

"The wise are neither young nor old—their physical age tells us nothing, and more than the generality of men can be divided between age and youth on the basis of their knowledge. The wise are always young in will and energy and old in experience and reflection." — Frances Lischner

Daniel

Daniel was a governmental officer and prophet of God (Daniel 1:1-6 and Matthew 24:15). As a young Jew, he was taken captive and trained for service in the Babylonian royal court. He served in influential positions under four kings—Nebuchadnezzar, Belshazzar, Darius, and Cyrus. He firmly refused to do anything contrary to God's teachings, even when it meant risking his life (Daniel 1:8 and 6:7-16). Daniel's gift of prophecy was evidenced early in life as his name means *God is my judge.*

The Old Testament Book of Daniel depicts Daniel's loyalty to God in the face of imprisonment, pagan religion, and false teaching. It also includes Daniel's visions. He was frequently pushed to compromise his faith, but he did not. His well-known choices include insisting on eating a healthy diet (chapter 1), worshiping God rather than avoiding the fiery furnace (chapter 3), interpreting the writing on the wall (chapter 5), and praying to God rather than avoiding the lion's den (chapter 6).

The last portion of the book—chapters 7 through 12—records visions God gave to Daniel that described Israel's future. This portion of Daniel is apocalyptic literature; it tells about the future with symbols and signs. These passages give hope that the cruelty would end and God's triumph would become obvious. Because Daniel showed his faith, Kings Nebuchadnezzar and Darius honored God.

Titus

Titus was a Greek Christian coworker with the Apostle Paul, who may have converted him to Christ (Titus 1:4). He traveled on missionary journeys with Paul and took Paul's first letter to the

Corinthians with the assignment of helping the church correct its problems (2 Corinthians 7:13-15).

The New Testament Book of Titus is a book of encouragement in the face of opposition, from Paul to Titus. As a means to urge him to seek Christian leaders with good character and to show him how to teach, in the book, Paul reminds Titus to hold onto sound faith and sound doctrine.

Timothy

Timothy was a native of Lystra who learned the Scriptures from his Jewish mother Eunice and grandmother Lois (Acts 16:1 and 2 Timothy 1:5). His father was a Greek. Timothy means *honoring God,* which he did as he served alongside The Apostle Paul, who was his father in the faith (1 Timothy 1:2). Timothy accompanied Paul on missionary journeys and was listed along with Paul in the sending of six letters—

- Second Corinthians
- Philippians
- Colossians
- First Thessalonians
- Second Thessalonians and
- Philemon.

The New Testament Books of Timothy were books Paul wrote to a young Christian coworker named Timothy. First Timothy warns against false teaching. It also gives instructions for church worship, presents characteristics of church leaders, and encourages Christian service. Second Timothy, written near the end of Paul's life, gives encouraging advice to Timothy including how to endure and to serve Christ faithfully.

Take Heed to Wise Counsel

We gain insight when we listen to those who have gone before and have experienced what we may be facing. Denying that others know more than we do is insight missed because we allow our pride to stand in the way. When we humble ourselves and acknowledge how little we really know, we are able to learn from others. Willingness to learn is a mark of those who are truly wise.

Consider Our Lord as a boy, "sitting in the midst of teachers, both listening to them and asking them questions" (Luke 2:46). Proverbs 1:5 says, *"A wise man will hear and increase learning, and a man of understanding will attain wise counsel."* If you think you know everything, you have a lot to learn. Even Jesus increased in wisdom.

"And Jesus increased in wisdom and stature, and in favor with God and man." (Luke 2:52)

BE PREPARED FOR JOB UNCERTAINTY

Reinventing yourself professionally does not necessarily mean changing jobs. You can make strategic moves without leaving your job. While on the job, ask yourself what do you want to do in your current job. Go ahead and explore the following options:

- Join professional organizations in your industry.
- Enlist a career coach or counselor to help you with your career move.
- Volunteer to serve on outside organizations, especially when it improves skills that will be noticeable back on the job.[11]

---

[11] The Sunday *Star Ledger Newspaper*, "Taking the Plunge, Ditching Corporate Life? Think Swan Dive, Not Belly-Flop," by Peter Genovese, October 20, 2002.

10 Tips for Job Seekers

1. **Gauge your finances** and build reserves to survive six months of unemployment.

2. **Don't take the first job** that comes your way out of desperation. However, consider taking a temporary job to get through the financial times.

3. **Sign up for unemployment** right away.

4. **Take advantage of COBRA** health insurance coverage.

5. **Keep your skills up to date**. There are government-funded nonprofit agencies that offer free retraining.

6. **Don't get down on yourself**. There's a mourning period after a layoff, which most people don't expect. But remember, layoffs are not the fault of the workers. After the massive growth of the late '90s, layoffs were inevitable. If you can afford it, take a brief vacation.

7. **Keep yourself on a schedule**. Set your alarm clock, go to the gym, surf the Web for job listings, work on your resume, meet friends for coffee. If you have a routine, that's going to spur your momentum.

8. **Separate your past from your future**. If you go into an interview feeling angry about your last situation, that will come through in the interview. If need be, take an hour before meeting with a potential employer to think about how you can add value to that company.

9. **Take advantage of outplacement services** offered by your former employer. They're free services that can be very valuable. You need to get yourself ready to be competitive. You're entering boot camp.

10. **Don't spam potential employers**. Sending out 700 resumes and form letters is not the way to go. Personalize your resume and cover letters to highlight the strengths each employer is seeking.[12]

---

[12] "Layoff Lessons Learned" by Allison Hemming, *ComputerWorld News* (February 19, 2002).

ANOMINITY BREEDS CONTENTMENT

Be content with who you are from the inside out. Do not seek fame from men. These are personal experiences. Reflect on the significant actions of the following unnamed Biblical characters and how they connect to your salvation experience:

It's better to be faithful than famous. David's soldiers found a young man who had been left behind by a retreating enemy army. The Egyptian slave is not named, but he provided key information that helped David to rescue his family.

"And David said unto him, To whom belongest thou? And whence art thou? And he said, I am a young man of Egypt, servant to an Amalekite; and my master left me, because three days agone I fell sick." (1 Samuel 30:13)

The young boy whose lunch of bread and fish was multiplied by Jesus to feed the thousands.

"There is a lad here, which hath five barley loaves, and two small fishes: but what are they among so many?" (John 6:9)

The owner of the colt on which Jesus rode into Jerusalem.

"And as they were loosing the colt, the owners thereof said unto them, Why loose ye the colt?" (Luke 19:33)

The owner of the house in which Jesus and His disciples ate the Passover.

"And ye shall say unto the Goodman of the house, The Master saith unto thee, Where is the guestchamber, where I shall eat the Passover with my disciples?" (Luke 22:11)

The boy who saved Paul's life.

"And when Paul's sister's son heard of their lying in wait, he went and entered into the castle, and told Paul. Then Paul called one of the centurions unto him, and said, Bring this young man unto the chief captain: for he hath a certain thing to tell him. So he took him, and brought him to the chief captain, and said, Paul the prisoner called me unto him, and prayed me to bring this young man unto

thee, who hath something to say unto thee. Then the chief captain took him by the hand, and went with him aside privately, and asked him, What is that thou hast to tell me? And he said, The Jews have agreed to desire thee that thou wouldest bring down Paul tomorrow into the council, as though they would enquire somewhat of him more perfectly. But do not thou yield unto them: for there lie in wait for him of them more than forty men, which have bound themselves with an oath, that they will neither eat nor drink till looking for a promise from thee. So the chief captain then let the young man depart, and charged him, See thou tell no man that thou hast shewed these things to me." (Acts 23:16-22)

FOOD FOR THOUGHT ON MATURITY

REMEMBER:

We judge ourselves by our beliefs and intentions, but others judge us by our behaviors and actions.

Police Officer

Construction Worker

Bus Driver

Computer Technician

Entrepreneur

Author

Nurse

PART II

The Journeyman Years...
From Learning to Leading

"Now after the death of Moses the servant of the LORD it came to pass, that the LORD spake unto Joshua the son of Nun, Moses' minister, saying, Moses my servant is dead; now therefore arise, go over this Jordan, thou, and all this people, unto the land which I do give to them, even to the children of Israel. Every place that the sole of your foot shall tread upon, that have I given unto you, as I said unto Moses…There shall not any man be able to stand before thee all the days of thy life; as I was with Moses, so I will be with thee: I will not fail thee, nor forsake thee. Be strong and of a good courage: for unto this people shalt thou divide for an inheritance the land, which I sware unto their fathers to give them. Only be thou strong and very courageous, that thou mayest observe to do according to all the law, which Moses my servant commanded thee: turn not from it to the right hand or to the left, that thou mayest prosper whithersoever thou goest." **(Joshua 1:1-3,5-7)**

*T*ransition from a state of learning to leading can be the most challenging—as well as most rewarding—portion of one's career. This state requires a different set of challenges, rules, policies, expectations, and values. Preoccupation with *self* must be substituted with a desire to make a positive and constructive impact on your surrounding—*others*. This means to help others achieve their goals while continually striving to improve the workplace for the benefit of everyone.

God handpicked Joshua as Moses' successor (Numbers 27) to lead the people of Israel into The Promised Land, Canaan. God Himself encouraged Joshua because he did not feel he could handle this awesome task. Through three major military campaigns involving more than thirty enemy armies, the people of Israel learn a crucial lesson under Joshua's leadership. Victory comes through faith in God and obedience to His Word rather than through superior numbers or military might. His comforting words in chapter one of the Book of Joshua, "...*be strong and of good courage*" (verse 6), are very appropriate during this transitional stage in the life of the worker.

In order to effectively apply what has been learned at the entry level, be guided at all times by God's word—"*Thy word is a lamp unto my feet, and a light onto my path.*" (Psalm 119:105) God encourages us to "*Acknowledge Him in all thy ways, and He shall direct thy paths.*" (Proverbs 3:6) The word "paths" is plural, and indicative of all of the options that we will have throughout our working life. Options lead to choices. Knowing that we will be faced with many, many options, we must not lean on our own understanding, but "trust in The Lord with all of your heart" (Proverbs 3:5). God is not in the business of disappointing His chosen children!

Having trusted fully in God, The Apostle Paul teaches us to extend kindness and courtesy to everyone, especially to our brothers and sisters in Christ. Our *light*—our lifestyle—could be the magnet that eventually draws others to Christ. We are the substance of things hoped for and the evidence that proclaims that God is real although He cannot be seen with the naked eye. *"Be kindly affectioned one to another with brotherly love; in honour preferring one another; Not slothful in business; fervent in spirit; serving the Lord; Rejoicing in hope; patient in tribulation; continuing in prayer."* (Romans 12:10-12) Love never fails because God is love (1 John 4:8).

Lastly, as we transition from learning to leading, we must be watchful as God's chosen overseers on the job. In our new and expanded role, we are responsible to be on alert and watch for situations and circumstances that we can change. *"Ye are all children of light, and the children of the day: we are not of the night, nor of darkness. Therefore let us not sleep, as do others; but let us watch and be sober."* (1 Thessalonians 5:5-6)

Be prayerful and vigilant. Show compassion, care, and understanding. Mediate where needed. Solve problems and make decisions based upon God's Word. Demonstrate the peace that passes all understanding while in the midst of tests, temptations, and trials. Dare to launch out into the deep! (Luke 5:4)

Chapter Four

Applying What You Now Know

"I just want to take common sense to higher places"—Reverend Jesse L. Jackson, Sr., United States Presidential candidate, during his keynote address to the elected delegates at the Democratic National Convention, 1988.

"Thy word is a lamp unto my feet, and a light onto my path." **(Psalm 119:105)**

Put into practice what you have learned.

*I*n the Book of Joshua, chapter one, the story of the transition in leadership from Moses to Joshua unfolds. Moses had been chosen by God to lead the children of Israel out of the wilderness and into the land that flowed with milk and honey. Through trials and errors, the children of Israel took forty years to travel a distance that should have taken only eleven days. The next generation is led by Moses' successor, Joshua, whose name means "The Lord Is Salvation." In the original Greek translation, his name takes on the form *Isous*, the same name borne by our Lord, Jesus. The final account of Joshua succeeding Moses is referenced in the book of Deuteronomy 34:10, which confirms Joshua's Godly appointment inasmuch as stating, *"And there arose not a prophet since in Israel like unto Moses, whom The LORD knew face to face."* This Book of Joshua records events that span forty years. It is considered the first of the Historical Books of the English Bible, because it traces the record of the children of Israel from the shores of The Jordan River to the conquest and division of the land of Canaan.

Chapter One begins *"Now after the death of Moses the servant of the LORD it came to pass, that the LORD spake unto Joshua the son of Nun, Moses' minister, saying..."* Joshua was Moses' assistant and servant (Exodus 24:13) and successor (Numbers 27:15-23). He served as a military field commander (Exodus 17:9-13), was a spiritual disciple of Moses when he accompanied him up the mountain to receive the Torah (Exodus 24:13), and acted as a believing, courageous spy along with Caleb (Numbers 14:6-10, 30). As Israel's new leader after Moses, Joshua functioned as a military commander taking the land of Canaan and as an administrator in allotting the land. He was a role model for all of Israel's future kings.

He was a leader possessing The Lord's spirit and having prophetic sanction (Numbers 27:18 and 22). He was both a military genius and a spiritual giant. He stirred up the faith of his army by ceremony (4:1-7), word (10:25), and life (24:15). He demanded of them exact obedience to The Lord's Word (Joshua 8:35 and 23:6). He lived to be 110 years of age. Furthermore, his acts are noteworthy in The New Testament in the Book of Acts (7:45). His excellent example of work in the ministry is an inspiration to those who study exactly how this man's steps were continually directed by the Lord.

"A man's heart deviseth his way: but The LORD directeth his steps." (Proverbs 16:9)

The LORD is sovereign over man's scheming and planning.

"Go to now, ye that say, To day or to morrow we will go into such a city, and continue there a year, and buy and sell, and get gain: Whereas ye know not what shall be on the morrow. For what is your life? It is even a vapour, that appeareth for a little time, and then vanisheth away. For that ye ought to say, If The Lord will, we shall live, and do this, or that. But now ye rejoice in your boastings: all such rejoicing is evil. Therefore to him that knoweth to do good, and doeth it not, to him it is sin." (James 4:13-17)

Do not pretend, or think, to know something that you do not. Do not presume to have the resources that you do not. God does have something for Christians to do and we should plan accordingly. We must include God in our plans. Omitting Him is not simply bad planning, it is sin.

What we do (achieve) is God's will, not our efforts. Although we need to plan and live responsibly, we are wise to recognize that ultimately, God has control. He is all-powerful (omnipotent), occupies all space (omnipresent), and infinite in knowledge (omniscient). Our unknown future is safe in the hands of The All-Knowing God.

Like Joshua, the military man, if we are going to avoid giving too much or too little attention to our work, we need to recognize the other elements of life that deserve our time. In the book *Your Work Matters to God* (NavPress), Doug Sherman and William Hendricks mention five parts of life that need our attention. They use the analogy of the sporting event called the pentathlon. In order for an athlete to do well, he must excel in running, swimming, horseback riding, pistol shooting, and fencing. The competitor cannot do well if he focuses on one event at the expense of others, or if he ignores any event. In a similar way, we must devote effort to five basic areas of life if we are to succeed at living as God desires. The five areas are:

Our personal life
Our family
Our church life
Our work
Our community life

READY FOR THE TRANSITION? DON'T WORRY

Why do we work? Some do it for love. Others do it for money. But most do it because we have no other choice. Today, our society is dominated by work not seen since The Industrial Revolution. Technology has offered increasing productivity and increased the standard of living for many. Conversely, bank tellers and typists have been replaced by machinery. Employment surveys of today's workers show a decline in job satisfaction. The biggest is in workload and workers feel crushed. The advent of technology brought faxes, cell phones, and ever-present email that have blurred the lines between home and work. Our jobs penetrate every aspect of life. Technology has given us more freedom but has also caused work to engulf and occupy us around the clock. "The work ethic and identifying ourselves with work and through work is not alive and well but more present now than at any time in history," says Rutgers University historian John Gillis.

It is beginning to take a toll. One third of America's workers—who work longer hours than their counterparts in any industrialized country—feel overwhelmed by the amount of work they have to do, according to The 2001 Families and Work Institute. In fact, of those surveyed, both men and women wish they were working about eleven hours less per week. However, they do not act upon it, as they do not want to be perceived as 'less committed.' Even the results from the 1973 report entitled, "Work in America," by The Department of Health, Education, and Welfare, a significant number of Americans were dissatisfied with the quality of their working lives. After decades of abundance, they still did not experience job satisfaction. Dull, repetitive, seemingly meaningless tasks, offering little challenge or autonomy, were causing discontent among workers at all occupational levels. Always a source of pride, the idea that hard work was a calling from God dated to The Reformation and the teachings of Martin Luther. While work had once been a means to serve God, two centuries of choices and industrialization had turned work into an end in itself, stripped of the spiritual meaning that sustained The Puritans who came ready to tame the wilderness.[13]

Consider the following insights on stress in the workplace:
- U.S. employers reportedly spend $150 to $200 billion annually on stress.
- 44 percent of office workers say stress on the job has worsened over the past two years.
- 52 percent of Americans say work is the main cause of stress in their lives.
- One out of five workers worldwide admit taking time off from work due to stress.[14]

---

[13] *U.S. News and World Report*, February 2003

[14] **A Survival Guide to The Stress of Organizational Change**, Price Pritchett and Ron Pound, 1995.

Mathematically speaking, it doesn't make sense to worry. Psychologists tell us that roughly 30% of what we worry about never happens; another 30% has already happened; 12% is about unfounded health concerns and another 20% is about sweating the small stuff. A total of 92% is for no good reason at all. That leaves only 8% of what we worry about. There is a growing mountain of evidence to suggest that worry is the chief contributor to depression, nervous breakdowns, high blood pressure, heart attacks, and early death. Stress kills. I have never known a man to die from hard work, but I have known a lot who have died from worry. Take comfort in God's Word:

> *"Be careful for nothing: but in every thing by prayer and supplication with thanksgiving let your requests be made known unto God."* (Philippians 4:6)

Maturity eliminates fear. Don't worry about anything. The Lord's near presence leads Paul to forbid his readers from worrying. The solution to undue anxiety is prayer in everything, "in any matter of life." The way to be free of anxiety is to be prayerful about everything. While God is eager to hear our requests, they are to be accompanied with thanksgiving.

> *"Cast thy burden upon the LORD, and He shall sustain thee: He shall never suffer the righteous to be moved."*
>
> (Psalm 55:22)

God invites us to burden Him with what burdens us. The psalm is a prayer by one who is being unjustly harassed and who has been betrayed by a friend. The entire Psalm 55 contains a prayer of petition, a lament over the man's present woeful state, and an expression of trust in God (verse 22).

> *"What time I am afraid, I will trust in thee."* (Psalm 56:3)

Trusting God's faithfulness dispels our fearfulness. Psalm 56 is a confident prayer for help.

Relax, meditate upon God's Word, and make great strides to avoid these basic mistakes throughout your day:

Basic Mistake #1—EXPECT SOMEBODY ELSE TO REDUCE YOUR STRESS
Lesson: Put yourself in charge of managing the pressure.

Basic Mistake #2—DECIDE NOT TO CHANGE
Lesson: People waste far more emotional energy desperately hanging on to old habits and beliefs than it would take for them to embrace the changes.

Basic Mistake #3—ACT LIKE A VICTIM
Lesson: Accept fate, and move on. You are better off if you appear resilient and remain productive.

Basic Mistake #4—TRY TO PLAY A NEW GAME BY THE OLD RULES
Lesson: Don't try harder, try differently.

Basic Mistake #5—SHOOT FOR THE LOW-STRESS WORK SETTING
Lesson: Don't fall into the trap of believing there's such a thing as a low-stress organization that is on track to survive.

Basic Mistake #6—TRY TO CONTROL THE UNCONTROLLABLE
Lesson: It is a bad investment of our psychological energy.

Basic Mistake #7—CHOOSE YOUR OWN PACE OF CHANGE
Lesson: Keep in step with the organization's intended rate of change.

Basic Mistake #8—FAIL TO ABANDON THE EXPENDABLE
Lesson: Eliminate unnecessary steps, get rid of busywork, and unload activities that don't contribute enough to the organization's current goals.

Basic Mistake # 9—SLOW DOWN
Lesson: Speed up. Cover more ground. Put your faith in action.

Basic Mistake #10—BE AFRAID OF THE FUTURE
Lesson: The best insurance policy for tomorrow is to make the most productive use of today.

Basic Mistake #11—PICK THE WRONG BATTLES
Lesson: Pick battles big enough to master, small enough to win.

Basic Mistake #12—PSYCHOLOGICALLY UNPLUG FROM YOUR JOB
Lesson: High job commitment is a gift you should give to yourself!

Basic Mistake #13—AVOID NEW ASSIGNMENTS
Lesson: Reach for new assignments that broaden your experience base. One of the best techniques for stress prevention is to keep updating your skills so you are highly employable.

Basic Mistake #14—TRY TO ELIMINATE UNCERTAINTY AND INSTABILITY
Lesson: Develop a greater tolerance for constant changes in the game plan.

Basic Mistake #15—ASSUME "CARING MANAGEMENT" SHOULD KEEP US COMFORTABLE
Lesson: All things considered, trying to keep you comfortable could be the most cold-blooded management move of all.

"It's been difficult, Ray. Grooming my successor has left me with precious little time for myself."

From *The Wall Street Journal*—Permission, Cartoon Features Syndicate.

In his book entitled *Don't Sweat the Small Stuff at Work*, Dr. Richard Carlson articulates that we must accept the fact that there will always be someone mad at us at any given time during the workday. He says:

"This is a difficult concept to accept, particularly if you are a 'people pleaser,' or worse still, an approval seeker. Yet I've found that if you don't make peace with this virtual inevitability, it guarantees that you will spend a great deal of time struggling with one of the unfortunate realities of life—disappointment.

The fact that someone is virtually always going to be mad at or at least disappointed in you is inevitable because while you're busy trying to please one person, you're often disappointing someone else. Even if your intentions are entirely pure and positive, you simply can't be in two places at the same time. So, if two or more people want, need or expect something from you—and you can't do it all— someone is going to be left disappointed. When you have dozens or even hundreds of demands on your time, and requests being fired at you from all different directions, a certain number of balls are going to be dropped. Mistakes are going to be made."

> From the errors of others, a wise man corrects his own.

PLAN YOUR STEPS WISELY

Up to forty percent of federal workers may retire by 2006. As you work toward the point of retirement, you realize something bigger awaits you on the other side of the horizon. There are more complex jobs you can handle. You have demonstrated an ability to learn, grow, develop, and to handle important situations in a mature manner. Promotion appears imminent. It is now time to *walk in what you now know*. For starters, recognize and acknowledge that in this society, the success of a company is directly tied to its ability to generate revenue. In 2002, nine of the world's eleven largest public companies were based in the United States:

Company	Market Value
General Electric	$245,254B
Microsoft	$235,266B
Wal-Mart Stores	$217,771B
Exxon Mobil	$215,562B
Pfizer	$179,624B
Johnson & Johnson	$160,906B
BP (UK)	$150,164B
Citigroup	$150,057B
American Internat'l Group	$142,805B
Royal Dutch/Shell (Netherlands/UK)	$142,151B
Coca-Cola	$119,052B[15]

In *The 1992–2005 Job Outlook in Brief*, published by United States Department of Labor, Bureau of Labor Statistics, it was predicted that significant job growth would occur in certain career fields over a fifteen-year period. While some predictions have come to fruition, for a variety of reasons, others have not. Predictions for the higher percentage change in various fields were as follows:

Executive, Administrative, and Managerial Occupations
    Construction contractors and managers   47%
Professional Specialty Occupations
    Metallurgical, ceramic, materials engineers 28%
—Computer, mathematical, and operations research occupations
    Computer scientists and systems analysts   111%
—Life sciences
    Lawyers and judges   28%
—Social scientists and Urban planners
    Psychologists   48%

---

[15] *The Wall Street Journal* Market Data Group

—**Social and recreation workers**
    Human services workers   136%
—**Teachers, librarians, and counselors**
    Teachers (K, Elementary, and Secondary)   34%
—**Health Diagnosing Occupations**
    Podiatrists   37%
—**Health Assessment and treating occupations**
    Physical therapists   88%
—**Communications Occupations**
Public relations specialists   26%
    Reports and correspondents   26%
—**Visual arts occupations**
    Photographers and camera operators   25%
—**Performing arts occupations**
    Actors, directors, producers   54%
Technicians and Related Support Occupations
    Radiologic technologists   63%
—**Technicians except health**
    Paralegals   86%
Marketing and Sales Occupations
    Travel agents   66%
Administrative Support Occupations Including Clerical
    Teacher aides   43%
Service Occupations
—**Protection service occupations**
    Correction officers   70%
—**Food and beverage preparation**
    Chefs, cooks, and other kitchen workers   38%
—**Health service occupations**
    Medical assistants   71%
—**Personal service and cleaning occupations**
    Homemaker-Home health aides   136%

Agriculture, Forestry, Fishing, and Related Occupations

    Fishers, hunters, and trappers   5%

Mechanics, Installers, and Repairers

    Automotive body repairers   30%

Construction Trades and Extractive Occupations

    Insulation workers   40%

Production Occupations

—Assemblers

    Blue-collar worker supervisors   12%

—Food procession occupations

    Butchers and meat, poultry, and fish cutters 3%

—Metalworking and plastics-working occupations

    Jewelers   19%

—Plant and systems operators

    Water and wastewater treatment
plant operators   18%

—Printing occupations

    Printing press operators   20%

—Textile, apparel, and furnishings occupations

    Upholsterers   11%

—Miscellaneous production occupations

    Ophthalmic laboratory technicians   22%

Transportation and Material Moving Occupations

    Truck drivers   26%

Handlers, Equipment Cleaners, Helpers, and Laborers   17%

If there is a way to achieve greatness, it can be done. Your talent is God's gift to you. What you do with it is your gift back to God.

"Every good gift and every perfect gift is from above, and cometh down from the Father of lights, with whom is no variableness, neither shadow of turning." (James 1:17)

Recognize and acknowledge the following: God is The Father, or Creator, of the heavenly bodies; As Our Creator, He is certainly more stable than us. With God, there is no change and He is immutable; God alone is good. This last principle relates to verse 17.

> *"For do I now persuade men, or God? Or do I seek to please men? For if I yet pleased men, I should not be the servant of Christ."* (Galatians 1:10)

Be a servant of Christ, don't try to please men. Never allow somebody else's approval to become your goal. Don't try to prove your value to men within society and the world. They may never see your good qualities. To deal effectively with others, you must be able to work alongside them—without allowing yourself to be controlled by their moods, or governed by their opinion of you.

> *"Seest thou a man diligent in his business? He shall stand before kings; he shall not stand before mean men."* (Proverbs 22:29)

Hard workers get rich. Skilled workers are always in demand and admired. For example, Nehemiah started out as a waiter but ended up rebuilding the whole city of Jerusalem.

> *"And they that be wise shall shine as the brightness of the firmament; and they that turn many to righteousness as the stars for ever and ever."* (Daniel 12:3)

Allow your *light* to shine brightly as a means to "attract" others toward the goodness of God Almighty!

Workplace Information To Know

What Employers Monitor

The most common ways employers check up on their employees:

Monitor internet use—21%

Review e-mail—16%

Eavesdrop on phone conversations—13%

Monitor use of online training program—8%

Record phone conversations—6%

Review voice mail—5%

Video—4%[16]

Ghost Work

"Ghost work" is a term that refers to the extra work required by staff during an economic downturn. Many executives face difficult challenges during these times, managing the leaner, morale-damaged staffs that remain after layoffs and cost-cutting measures. They still have to get the same amount of work done despite the shrinking staff and resources.

Inevitably, these bosses have to ask their employees to do not only their regular jobs but also the work of axed colleagues—and without additional pay. The result is that no one gets the training needed to do this 'ghost work,' or the jobs of departed colleagues. The problem with 'ghost work' is that employees not only have more work to do but aren't very efficient at it since they may not have the knowledge they need to do it well. The only option is to work smarter.

The 'ghost work' employees must do makes them feel less-than-grateful to survive job cuts. From the boss' point of view, the survivors are supposed to feel lucky that they have jobs, but instead they feel they're working even harder than ever—and can only see that they need attention, encouragement, and help. Things that they are not getting in the workplace![17]

---

[16] *Sales & Marketing Management Magazine* survey of 500 executives, USA TODAY SNAPSHOTS®, by Darryl Haralson and Quin Tian.

[17] *The Wall Street Journal*, Marketplace Section, "Getting a Lean Staff to Do 'Ghost Work' of Departed Colleagues," October 22, 2002, by Carol Hymowitz.

Work-Life Trends to Watch

There is a slowing growth trend in flexible scheduling at work. Consider the percentage of workers with flexible schedules:

1991	15.1%
1997	27.6%
2001	28.8%

The number of families that utilize technology at home is growing rapidly (number of U.S. telecommuters):

2002	9.1 million
2003	9.3 million[18]

Test Your Stress Level

*Circle all of the events that have occurred in your life over the past 12 to 18 months. Total your **Life Change Units** (LCUs). LCUs are in bold that are specific to the workplace.

1. Death of spouse	100
2. Divorce	73
3. Marital separation	65
4. **Jail term**	63
5. Death of a close family member	63
6. Personal injury or illness	53
7. Marriage	50
8. **Fired from job**	47
9. Marital reconciliation	45
10. **Retirement**	45
11. Change in health of a family member	44
12. Pregnancy	40

---

[18] U.S. Administration on Aging: Center for Designing Work Wisely and the Economic Policy Institute; IDC, Framington, MA.

13. Sex difficulties	39	
14. Gain of new family member	39	
15. **Business readjustment**	39	
16. **Change in financial state**	38	
17. Death of close friend	37	
18. **Change to different line of work**	36	
19. Change in the number of arguments with spouse	35	
20. Loan for major purchase	31	
21. Foreclosure of loan/mortgage	30	
22. **Change in responsibilities at work**	29	
23. Son or daughter leaving home	29	
24. Trouble with in-laws	29	
25. **Outstanding personal achievement**	28	
26. **Spouse begins or stops work**	26	
27. Begin or end school	26	
28. **Change in living conditions**	25	
29. **Revision of personal habits**	24	
30. **Trouble with boss**	23	
31. **Change in work hours or conditions**	20	
32. **Change in residence**	20	
33. Change in schools	20	
34. Change in recreation	19	
35. Change in church activities	19	
36. Change in social activities	18	
37. Loan for a lesser purchase	17	
38. Change in sleeping habits	16	

39. Change in number of family get-togethers   15

40. Change in eating habits   15

41. **Vacation**   13

42. Holidays   12

43. Minor violations of the law   11

0 – 150 LCUs: your level of stress based on life change is low

150 – 300 LCUs: borderline stress level…you should attempt to minimize changes in your life at this time

Over 300 LCUs: your stress levels are high…you should minimize changes in your life and institute some stress intervention techniques.[19]

---

[19] American Massage Therapy Association brochure

FOOD FOR THOUGHT ON APPLYING WHAT YOU KNOW

I Now Know That:

1. During the early 1900's. 85% of our workers were in agriculture. Now agriculture involves less than 3% of the workforce.
2. In 1950, 73% of U.S. employees worked in production or manufacturing. Now less than 15% do.
3. The Department of Labor estimated that by the year 2000 at least 44% of all workers would be in data services (gathering, processing, retrieving, or analyzing information).
4. Careers come and go. Jobs change. This is nothing new—it is just happening much faster than ever before.
5. Work is going global. We have entered *The Information Age.* The economy is shifting more and more toward *services*, and toward *knowledge work*. Knowledge has become our most important 'product.'
6. The world does not care about our opinions or feelings. The world only rewards those of us who catch on to what's happening, who invest our energy in finding and seizing the opportunities brought about by change.
7. In 1991, for the first time ever, companies spent more money on computing and communications gear than the combined monies spent on industrial, mining, farm, and construction equipment.
8. Since 1983, the U.S. work world has added 25 million computers. The number of cellular telephone subscribers has jumped from zero in 1983 to 16 million by the end of 1993.
9. Communication technology is radically changing the speed, direction, and amount of information flow, even as it alters work roles all across organizations. As a case in point, the number of secretaries is down 521,000 since 1987.
10. A weekday edition of *The New York Times* contains more information than the average person in 17th-century England was likely to come across in a lifetime.
11. Today's average consumers wear more computing power on their wrists than existed in the entire world before 1961.
12. During the decade of the 1980's, a total of 230 companies— 46%—disappeared from The "Fortune 500." Obviously, size does not guarantee continued success. Neither does a good reputation.

Chapter Five

Become What You Have Learned

"Dare to believe that God does love you. Believe it against all odds. Dream against all dreams that God does care about you and has a plan for your life and wants you to succeed."
—Dr. Robert A. Schuller, Senior Pastor, The Crystal Cathedral, Garden Grove, California

"Be kindly affectioned one to another with brotherly love; in honour preferring one another; Not slothful in business; fervent in spirit; serving the Lord; Rejoicing in hope; patient in tribulation; continuing in prayer."
(Romans 12:10-12)

Cultivate your skills with patience.
Be fair and cordial as you progress.

*D*r. Robert H. Schuller started a church in 1955 with 100 members in a drive-in theater. Today, he runs a multi-million-member ministry and can be seen on a weekly worldwide broadcast entitled, *"Hour of Power."* From his boyhood on a poor Iowa farm, he became a counselor to United States Presidents and an inspiring voice to millions. Even though he was born in a house at the dead end of an unnamed dirt road, Dr. Schuller challenges us all to become what we have learned through his inspiring words—*"If you can dream it, you can do it."*

In his book, **My Journey**, Dr. Schuller gives an account of his humble beginnings. His journey began in a home with no electricity and no proper running water. After graduating from college and entering Western Theological Seminary, he realized that as long as you have a burning desire and a dream, you can go anywhere from nowhere. In the book, Dr. Schuller recalls that on September 14, 1980, a donated organ's music filled the space of the world's largest all-glass auditorium—The Crystal Cathedral.[20]

WE ARE RESPONSIBLE AND ACCOUNTABLE TO GOD

Small kindnesses, small courtesies, small considerations, habitually practiced in our social intercourse give a greater charm to the character than the display of great talents and accomplishments (Mary Ann Kelly). The people who make a difference in your life are not the ones with the most credentials, the most money, or the most awards. They are the ones who *care.* God's Word says, *"But the path of the just is as the shining light, that shineth more and more unto the perfect day."* (Proverbs 4:18) Effective teaching comes only through a changed person. When you stop changing, you stop

---

[20] *Parade Magazine*, "If you can dream it, You can do it," by Robert H. Schuller October, 21, 2001. pgs.14-16).

leading. Because The Apostle Paul was forced to spend all but seven years of his ministry in prison, we get to read his life-changing epistles 2000 years later. His work attests to the fact that the greatest risk of all is to risk nothing.

> *If not you, who? If not now, when?*
> *—Abraham Maslow*

Responsibility

One of the most popular scriptures in *The Holy Bible* describes the awesome principles of stewardship and responsibility. *"For unto whomsoever much is given, of him shall be much required: and to whom men have committed much, of him they will ask the more,"* is found in The Book of Luke (12:48). It stresses the heavy responsibility of servants, as followers of Jesus are supposed to be. The word "responsibility" represents the state, quality, or fact of being responsible. It is derived from two words—*response* and *ability*. It is a measure of our ability to respond to a given situation, circumstance, or stewardship. In expanding on this matter, Jesus teaches us a valuable lesson about responsibility in verses 41 through 48. He teaches that the faithful and wise steward is blessed and will be made a ruler over all that he has. The unfaithful servant, however, is punished in four ways: The Lord will not look for him, He will cut him into two, He will appoint his portion with the unbelievers, and he shall be beaten with many stripes!

> *"But He that knew not, and did commit things worthy of stripes, shall be beaten with few stripes. For unto whomsoever much is given, of him shall be much required: and to whom men have committed much, of him they will ask the more."* (Luke12: 48)

> *"But thou, O man of God, flee these things; and follow after righteousness, godliness, faith, love, patience, meekness."*
> (1 Timothy 6:11)

"Flee these things" means "shun a love for money (verse 10) and the striving for material wealth with all of their resulting woes." To "follow after" means "to pursue." Righteousness is practical correctness, conforming to God's will in our thinking and acting. Godliness is proper reverence—holding in fear— and being obedient to God. Faith is a trust in God that grows stronger. Love is a maturing affection for God and man. Patience is perseverance or steadfastness in life and service. Meekness, or gentleness, translates as power under control.

You and I are entrusted with a high degree of responsibility as Christians. We are 'Christ-like ones'—*christos*—ambassadors for Christ, and are instructed to be living epistles. God trusts that we will fulfill the purpose for which we were born and carry out His mandate, *"To seek and to save that which was lost."* Where we work is prime territory to win souls for Christ. New opportunities are presented to us daily to demonstrate the love of Christ. Examples of faithful living on the job, we are the substance of things hoped for and the evidence that there is a God in which people can put their trust even when they cannot see Him.

We should greet all people each morning with a big smile and a gesture of "Good Morning!" Allow the love of The Lord to be visible throughout the workday. Take your responsibility seriously. Win souls for Christ while earning an honest day's wage. The following scriptures are God's plan for us to obey, adhere, and implement in our lives:

Genesis 4:9—*"And the LORD said unto Cain, Where is Abel thy brother? And he said, I know not: Am I my brother's keeper?"*

Proverbs 24:11-12—*"If thou forbear to deliver them that are drawn unto death, and those that are to be slain; If thou sayest, Behold, we knew it not, doth not he that pondereth the heart consider it? And he that keepeth thy soul, doth not he know it? And shall not he render to every man according to his works?"*

John 10:12-13—*"But he that is an hireling, and not the shepherd, whose own the sheep are not, seeth the wolf coming, and leaveth the sheep, and fleeth: and the wolf catcheth them, and scattereth the sheep. The hireling fleeth, because he is an hireling, and careth not for the sheep."*

Acts 18:6—*"And when they opposed themselves, and blasphemed, he shook his raiment, and said unto them, Your blood be upon your own heads; I am clean: from henceforth I will go unto the Gentiles."*

Romans 14:12—*"So then every one of us shall give account of himself to God."*

Galatians 6:5—*"For every man shall bear his own burden."*

1 Timothy 5:8—*"But if any provide not for his own, and specially for those of his own house, he hath denied the faith, and is worse than an infidel."*

Accountability

Accountability means to be responsible and answerable. With such an awesome responsibility of representing God, through Jesus Christ, in the earth, we will be held accountable for our actions as well as inactions. Accountability is derived from two words—*account* and *ability.* It signifies a willingness to accept the outcome of which we have been trusted to manage, oversee, or care for in general. In a sense, responsibility and accountability are inseparable. In the original Greek translation, accountability is derived from the word *kataxio*, or account, and it denotes "to account worthy" or "to judge worthy" as referenced in Luke 20:35 and 21:36. This verb is actually taken from two Greek words—*kata*—meaning "intensive" and *axios*—meaning "worthy." Another translation for the word "account" comes from *katischu*—and means "to prevail" (Acts 5:41) and "were counted worthy." (2 Thessalonians 1:5)

As we progress on our respective jobs, we are held to a higher standard concerning our overall responsibility. Likewise, the accountability factor stiffens and expectations increase. During the early years of our careers, we spend time learning about the new job and how to function within the team setting. Expectations are not unreasonably high at this point in time. But as we move into the next phase—team leader, manager, or senior office holder—we are held to a higher standard and higher accountability. It is expected that we will apply those things that we have learned through on-the-job training. Measurable results are now expected with minimal oversight. We will be held accountable for the results, either positively or negatively. Knowing this, Christians have a dual role on the job—to represent God according to His Word and to be excellent workers when it comes to the performance of their job. As we let our *light* so shine before men, we are obeying God's commandment and He will make provisions for us to excel in and on our jobs. We are, in essence, entrusted to raise the level of productivity of others around us. He will continually protect us from man's evil devices. He will strategically place the right people in our paths and open doors.

Upon further examination of the root word "account," we find it means to reckon, calculate, consider, let your mind dwell on, and to give reasons (for). In Matthew 12:36, Luke 16:2, and Romans 14:12, God's Word describes it as accepting responsibility for something. When someone is accounted, it is credited to or recognized as belonging to someone (Galatians 3:6 and Luke 22:24). Also, an account is a detailed record, count, or credit as referenced in Deuteronomy 2:11 and Psalm 144:3.

"Blessed is the man whose strength is in thee; in whose heart are the ways of them." (Psalm 84:5)

Be strong in the Lord while considering the concerns of others before your own.

"I believe supernatural forces are at work."

From *The Wall Street Journal*—Permission, Cartoon Features Syndicate.

Become What You Desire To See In Others

Ever hear of Edcouch, Elsa, or La Villa, Texas? In these tiny towns, 90% of the households have incomes of less than $10,000, and 91% of parents lack a high school diploma. Yet, in the last decade, Edcouch-Elsa High School has sent 45 students to elite colleges and universities such as Stanford, Brown, Yale and Princeton, while 65% of graduating students go on to some form of higher education— well above national norms for Hispanic students. More remarkable, many graduates choose to return to these towns to live, work and encourage others to achieve their goals. This commitment has nurtured a movement called "Place-Based Education," which takes the history, culture, economy and ecology of a community and uses them as a textbook and laboratory. Thus, the community becomes a classroom. Mr. Francisco "Frank" Guarjardo, a history teacher who helped found The Llano Grande Center at the high school says, "Our students don't inherit yachts, stores or stock options, but they live in a vibrant community with a wealth of human stories."

Today, communities across the nation are applying the place-based education techniques to teach a broad range of subjects, including science, history, geography, the arts and even math, in more than 700 rural elementary and secondary schools in 33 states, as follows:

Clinton and Jackson, Louisiana	Students analyzed water samples from creeks to determine the flow of pollutants.
Mendocino, California	Students restored a Chinese temple.
Sante Fe, New Mexico	Students interviewed Pueblo tribal elders about traditional growing cycles and plant remedies.
18 rural schools in Vermont	Students worked with community members to solve local problems.[21]

A one-man mission of mercy

Every Sunday at 1:30 P.M., rain or shine, Hector Perez can be found in the parking lot of the Bound Brook, New Jersey train station. Members of about 30 indigent families, most of them Hispanic immigrants, stand in line waiting for him. Without question, Mr. Perez provides bags of food and used clothes for the needy. The only requirement is that they sign their names in a notebook, proving that they received Mr. Perez's help. He is not affiliated with any agency such as the Red Cross or Salvation Army, or any church outreach groups that already serve the impoverished. Instead, he recognized the need of those who do not have transportation to the neighboring town's food bank and chose to get involved after Hurricane Floyd devastated the town in 1999. He delivered food from the food bank to flood victims and brought overstocked food from churches back to the food bank. Mr. Perez, who is unemployed,

---

[21] "When the Community is a Classroom," *Parade Magazine*, April 28, 2002, pg. 8.

became disabled when he injured his right arm while working at a plastics factory in Plainfield, New Jersey 14 years ago. "God gave me enough strength and the will to do this, so I am here," he said. "If I don't show up, then all these people have no food."[22]

Souper Bowl vs. Super Bowl

While many Americans are thinking about an evening in front of the television watching the most highly-anticipated football game of the year, a number of teenagers across the country will be marking Super Bowl Sunday in a different way. On the morning before the kickoff, Souper Bowl of Caring, an annual event that began thirteen years ago in Columbia, South Carolina, starts its day with approximately 15,000 church congregations across the country raising money for food pantries, soup kitchens, and other local efforts to help the disadvantaged. In New Jersey, for example, First Baptist Church in Westfield asked each of its members to throw a dollar into the soup pots, resulting in $300 to $400 in donation for the Community FoodBank of New Jersey. Not far away, 15 or 20 volunteers from the youth group of Connecticut Farms Presbyterian Church in Union stand in the entry after their 11:00 A.M. service to accept cash donations and non-perishable foods for the food pantry at their church. At St. John Neumann Roman Catholic Church Parish in Califon, junior high schoolers take responsibility for The Souper Bowl of Caring. As they remind the parishioners of this project, they collect money and cans of soup. The soup and approximately $550 collected is donated to a program that the teens choose. The students personally deliver the soup to a soup kitchen and spend a day in February or March volunteering.

Crescent Avenue Presbyterian Church in Plainfield said the money collected during Souper Bowl of Caring goes to the bag lunch program at the church, which feeds 36 people per day, five days per week. The high school youth group at St. Stephen's Lutheran Church in Edison

---

[22] "No One Goes Hungry If He Can Help It," *Sunday Star Ledger*, June 9, 2002, by Cathy Bugman, staff writer.

collects their monetary donations that go to the Lutheran World Hunger drive. Pastor Anna Kalandova says, "I think it's a good project for American kids. We want to involve them in social ministry."

Information on The Souper Bowl of Caring is available at: www.souperbowl.org or (800) 358-7687.[23]

TEST YOUR 'COMMON SENSE'

Take this test as a means of measuring how you would handle certain situations or respond to certain circumstances. At the end of the test, you will be able to measure your level of *common sense* based upon a scoring system that measures Intelligence Quotient (IQ). Remember, this is only a test. IQ tests only measure where you are today. The IQ test is not an accurate measure of your potential! Do not allow the results of any test to dictate your value or worth to God. Remember: You are fearfully and wonderfully made by Him and He loves you. You are only required to do what is pleasing in His sight and see yourself as God sees you. Everybody needs love. Always remember the lyrics of "Jesus Loves Me", written by Anna B. Warner (1824-1915). It's a popular song that is sung by children and adults around the world — *"Jesus loves me, this I know, for The Bible tells me so."* The cross of Jesus is supreme evidence of the love of God.

1. You are about to cross a busy intersection as you walk home, but the light is out of order. What should you do?
   a. Cross with caution
   b. Don't cross

2. Tuna is your favorite food, and you love all varieties equally. Today, you find the fancy grade on sale at half-price: Now it costs only twice as much as the unfancy grade. You're always short of cash. What should you do?

---

[23] "Hunger Drives Them," *Sunday Star Ledger*, January 19, 2003, by Patricia C. Turner, staff writer

a. Buy the fancy kind.
b. Buy the unfancy kind.

3. You need a warm winter coat, and you've found two on sale. One is twice as warm as the other, but the other one looks much better. Which should you buy?
a. The warmer one.
b. The one that looks better.

4. You should get a haircut before you go on a job interview tomorrow, but you don't have enough money. What should you do?
a. Go to the interview.
b. Cancel the interview.

5. Your favorite shoes are wearing out. They can be repaired as good as new for $50. A new pair costs $100. What should you do?
a. Repair the shoes.
b. Buy a new pair.

6. You're starting to take a test. One of the directions notes that there is a penalty for guessing. What should you do?
a. Guess.
b. Don't guess.

7. You're looking for an apartment and find two that you can afford. One has a view of the park. The other has a view of a flashing neon sign. Which apartment should you rent?
a. The one with the park view.
b. The one with the view of the flashing neon sign.

Note: Answers can be found in Appendix B.

IS WORK YOUR GOD?

Ultimately, we are working for the Lord. He is the boss' Boss, the supervisor's Supervisor, and foreman's Foreman, and the manager's Manager. *"And whatsoever ye do, do it heartily, as to the Lord, and not unto men."* (Colossians 3:23) The goal of work is not to gain wealth and possessions, but to serve the common good and bring glory to God.[24] Contrary to how we may feel sometimes, work itself is not a curse. When we learn to see it properly, we realize that in almost every job there is a way of working for and with God. We need to understand that the perfect life is not a work-free existence. Work was part of the Lord's blueprint for daily life in Paradise. When we accept God's perspective on work, we will find fulfillment.[25]

The ability to work is a wonderful gift, but are we taking it too far? There was a time, a generation ago, when people left their jobs at the office, but now, we come home to email and phone messages. God commands us in Exodus 20:3, *"You shall have no other gods before Me."* No matter what our occupation, we must keep work in perspective. God and family are more important than dedication to a job. Work is a gift, not a god. Honor God with everything you have. Give Him the first and the best. In 1 Thessalonians 4:11-12, we are instructed to *"...Study to be quiet, and to do your work with your own hands, as we commanded you. That ye may walk honestly toward them that are without, and that ye may have lack of nothing."* The goal is to win the respect of unbelievers. They need to see that your faith in Christ makes a positive difference in the practical, everyday aspects of your life. In the book of Titus, The Apostle Paul tells Titus that part of the motive workers should have is to *"Make the teaching about God our Savior attractive."* (2:10—NIV) An honest day's work backs up our profession of faith and points to the truth of The Gospel. Ecclesiastes says that life is short, wealth is fleeting, and one's relationship with God and people is more important than

---

[24] Richard Foster

[25] *How Can I Find Satisfaction in My Work?*, 1991 RBC Ministries-Grand Rapids, MI

any lesser concept of success. Likewise, the Book of Proverbs teaches us: *"Do not wear yourself out to get rich; have the wisdom to show restraint."* (Proverbs 23:4 NIV)

Dr. Dave Arnott, associate professor of management at Dallas Baptist University, says, "I do not know whether work is taking over family and community, or whether family and community are giving up their place to work. But I know the movement is going on. Everyone's job seems to be who they are." We tend to equate our identity with what we do for a living.

The president of the Families and Work Institute says, "How busy you are has become the red badge of courage…It has become a status symbol," even though people complain about it.[26] Our sense of personal worth is closely connected to a feeling that we are accomplishing something purposeful with our lives. Because of that, work and a satisfying life are inseparable. Unfortunately, work does not always give us that sense of satisfaction. Always remember— To show His love, Jesus died for us. To show our love, we must live for Him. Work for God, not man! Don't just make money, make an impact![27]

After all the complaints about how the workplace is never a meritocracy and how back-stabbers always win, now is the time for hard-working and trustworthy managers to present themselves as the new face of upper management.

With dozens of senior executives under scrutiny for wrongdoings, middle managers are "like kids in dysfunctional families," says Dory Hollander, a partner at WiseWorkplaces in Arlington, Virginia. "They're looking at the bosses they've depended on and saying, 'I don't want to be like them—and maybe I can do a whole lot better.'"

Middle managers often have more regular contact with customers, suppliers and employees than their top bosses, so they have a chance to show their integrity, the quality most desired in leaders today. Pat Cook, head of Cook & Co., a boutique executive search firm, says

---

[26] *Our Daily Bread*, February 21, 2003

[27] Attorney Willie Gary

that during the dot-com boom, youth, speed and exuberance were highly valued traits, but in the past few months, clients mostly want to know they can trust a candidate.

"We're back to basics where what counts is honesty and reliability, along with the ability to get hard-core results," she adds, "All those people who got ahead for all the wrong reasons are going to have to stand aside."[28]

IT'S OKAY TO GLORIFY GOD AT WORK

In the *Fortune* Magazine article by Marc Gunther entitled, "God & Business—Bringing Spirituality Into the Workplace Violates the Old Idea that Faith and Fortune Don't Mix. But a Groundswell of Believers is Breaching the Last Taboo in Corporate America," the author encourages each of us to work from our soul. This article focuses on a group of executives, most of them Catholic, who belong to a Chicago-area group called Business Leaders of Excellence, Ethics, and Justice. For more than a decade they have wrestled with big questions such as: How can business promote family life? What is a just wage? When are layoffs justified?

"Spirituality in the workplace is exploding," declares Laura Nash, a senior research fellow at Harvard Business School who has followed the topic for a decade. The move is on to make the workplace a more ethical and humane arena, one where believers and nonbelievers alike can find fulfillment. A similar article was published in 1953 by *Fortune* Magazine, entitled "Businessmen on Their Knees." The story noted that prayer groups were forming and that religious books were climbing up the bestseller lists, and asked, "Is it a superficial, merely utilitarian movement, or is it a genuinely spiritual awakening?" As Jose Zeilstra says, "Ultimately, I am working for God. There is no higher calling than to serve God, and

---

[28] "Middle Managers Find Their Skills, Integrity Now Carry More Weight," *The Wall Sreet Journal,* Marketplace Section, July 30, 2002, by Carol Hymowitz

that does not mean only within the church. Ultimately, your life—whether work, family, or friends—is part of a larger plan."

The ongoing question remains—How do we treat the migrant worker, the single mother, and the illegal immigrant? These are merely the modern-day equivalents of the biblical poor.

Background

The spiritual revival in the workplace reflects, in part, a broader religious reawakening in America, which remains one of the world's most observant nations. Depending on how the question is asked, as many as 95% of Americans say they believe in God. The Princeton Religious Research Index, which has tracked the strength of organized religion in America since World War II, reports a sharp increase in religious beliefs and practices since the mid-1990s. In 1999, The Gallup Poll asked Americans if they felt a need to experience spiritual growth. For the poll, 78% said 'yes,' up from 20% in 1994. Sales of Bibles and prayer books, inspirational volumes, and books about philosophy and Eastern religions are growing faster than any other category, with the market expanding from 1.69 billion dollars to about 2.24 billion dollars in the past five years, according to the Book Industry Study Group.

Psalm 118:8, which marks the center of *The Holy Bible*, reads, *"It is better to trust in the LORD than to put confidence in man."*

FOOD FOR THOUGHT ON LEARNING

People are successful not because of what they say, but because of what they ask.
                    —Attorney Johnnie L. Cochran, Jr.

Knowing is the enemy of learning…We've all got to be learners. Learners are people who are constantly questioning everything all the time, including, and with most difficulty, their own assumptions about what they know and what they don't know.   —Larry Wilson, founder and vice chairman,
                    Pecos River Division, AON Consulting

Seven reasons why questions stimulate learning:
   1. Questions demand answers.
   2. Questions stimulate thinking.
   3. Questions give us valuable information.
   4. Questions put you in control.
   5. Questions get people to open up.
   6. Questions lead to quality listening.
   7. Questions get people to persuade themselves.[29]

---

[29] ***The 7 Powers of Questions, Secrets to Successful Communication in Life and at Work,*** by Dorothy Leeds.

Chapter Six

What Makes a Leader?

"All that is necessary for evil to triumph is for good men to do nothing."
—Edmund Burke, January 9, 1795

"Ye are all children of light, and the children of the day: we are not of the night, nor of darkness. Therefore let us not sleep, as do others; but let us watch and be sober." **(1 Thessalonians 5:5-6)**

Service to others makes you a great leader.

*Y*ou may be only one person in the world, but you may also be the world to one person.[30] Our day's work is not done until we build up someone. God could send another flood, as He did in Noah's day, to cleanse away the wickedness of the world. He could, but He will not. He had promised never to do that again (Genesis 9:11). Instead, He chooses to work through human beings like us, changing us, then, in turn, enabling us to function as His agents of change.

Only the one who has learned to serve is qualified to lead. A leader is a servant. Care and concern for others is a key attribute of a successful leader. Leadership is about capturing the imagination and enthusiasm of your people with clearly defined goals that cut through the fog like a beacon in the night. I have read and studied multiple books on leadership. The various sources all lead to one common denominator—To be an effective leader, you must have followers. Christ-like leadership means considering the our neighbors needs before our own, seeking their good, encouraging their spiritual growth and setting the stage for their intimacy with God. It means treating others the way that God has treated us. Servant leaders employ gentle persuasion and reason rather than barking orders and ultimatums. Service for others is the basis of true greatness.

The word "leader," in its original Greek translation, has two meanings:

1. *agō*—"to bring, bear, carry, lead" is translated by the verb "to lead." The use of this version of "lead" is best captured in the following scriptures and is used metaphorically in Romans 2:4

---

[30] *Good Stuff,* January 2003

Mark 13:11—*"But when they shall **lead** you, and deliver you up, take no thought beforehand what ye shall speak, neither do ye premeditate: but whatsoever shall be given you in that hour, that speak ye: for it is not ye that speak, but The Holy Ghost."*

Luke 4:1—*"And Jesus being full of The Holy Ghost returned from Jordan, and was **led** by the Spirit into the wilderness."*

Jesus was directed where to go at a predetermined time by The Holy Spirit.

Luke 4:9—*"And he brought him into Jerusalem, and set him on a pinnacle of the temple, and said unto him, If thou be the Son of God, cast thyself down from hence."*

The higher parts of the temple stood next to a deep ravine. The elevation would have been considerable. Had Jesus performed this feat before the crowds below, He would certainly have attracted acclaim. But His steadfast aim remained obedience, not popularity.

Luke 22:54—*"Then took they him, and **led** him, and brought him into the high priest's house. And Peter followed afar off."*

Luke 23:1—*"And the whole multitude of them arose, and **led** him into Pilate."*

Luke 23:32—*"And there were also two others, malefactors, **led** with him to be put to death."*

John 18:28—*"Then **led** they Jesus from Caiaphas unto the hall of judgment: and it was early; and they themselves went not into the judgment hall, lest they should be defiled; but that they might eat the Passover."*

Acts 8:32—*"The place of the scripture which he read was this, HE WAS **LED** AS A SHEEP TO THE SLAUGHTER; AND LIKE A LAMB DUMB BEFORE HIS SHEARER, SO OPENED HE NOT HIS MOUTH."*

Romans 2:4—*"Or despiseth thou the riches of his goodness and forbearance and longsuffering; not knowing that the goodness of God **leadeth** thee to repentance?"*

2. *hodēgeō*—"to lead the way" and "guide" as used in Acts 1:16. It is used figuratively in the following scriptures:

Acts 1:16—*"...which was guide to them that took Jesus."*

Matthew 15:14—*"Let them alone: they be blinded leaders of the blind. And if the blind **lead** the blind, both shall fall into the ditch."*

Indicates ineffective leadership guides others to their ultimate destruction.

Matthew 23:16—*"Woe unto you, ye blind guides, which say, Whosoever shall swear by the temple, it is nothing; but whosoever shall swear by the gold of the temple, he is a debtor!"*

Matthew 23:24—*"Ye blind guides, which strain at a gnat, and swallow a camel."*

Romans 2:19—*"And art confident that thou thyself art a guide to the blind, a light of them which are in darkness."*

LEAD GOD'S WAY

Pastor John C. Maxwell, Ph.D., founded a leadership development institute in 1995 called INJOY. This institute is committed to increasing the effectiveness of people in all areas of life. Having studied his many books, Pastor Maxwell's writings and teachings focus on four primary areas that inspire **REAL** success:

- **R**elationships
- **E**quipping
- **A**ttitude
- **L**eadership

One of the most inspirational lessons I have learned from reading Pastor Maxwell's books is the principle of *'being a part of something greater than ourselves.'* This principle simply means that in order to live a worthwhile, meaningful life, we must live a life that has no temporary, but an eternal impact. In other words, we must strive to become the person that God has created us to be—to reach our potential. *"You motivate me to dream big dreams and trust God for the impossible,"* is one of the best compliments that any of us can receive from a subordinate, peer, colleague, friend, family member, or an associate.[31]

In his book entitled, ***The 108 Skills of Natural Born Leaders***, author Warren Blank defines 108 skills of successful leaders. He lists them in three categories as nine skill sets:

The Skills of Natural Born Leaders

Category	Skill Sets
Foundational skills	Expand self-awareness. Build rapport. Clarify expectations.
Leadership direction skills	Map the territory to identify the need to lead. Chart a course of leadership action. Develop others as leaders.
Leadership influence skills	Build the base to gain commitment. Influence others to willingly follow. Create a motivating environment.

Skills 61 (*Coach and Train*) and Skill 63 (*Appraise Continuously*) are particularly insightful in that they articulate the leaders' service to others. *Coach and Train* are one-to-one, face-to-

---

[31] Page 189—***Developing the Leaders Around You***, 1995. Thomas Nelson Publishers

face, day-to-day developmental activities. Coaching improves, extends, refines, or redirects behavior where a person already has some knowledge and skill. There are five successful coaching behaviors:

1. Tell people what they need to do to improve.
2. Show people how to improve.
3. Clarify the consequences of behavior.
4. Provide the big picture.
5. Use a confidence builder.

This involves good and on-going communication. Skill 63 is *Appraise Continuously*. Appraisal comes from the root word *praise*. Appraisal includes positive recognition and rewards for the full range of performance. The intent is to focus more on the person, not the specific project.

To *Appraise Continuously* is to concentrate on shaping employee's behavior, instead of grading people's behavior. Be a coach, not a judge or umpire. You personally may need to function more as a teacher, trainer or coach, and not just as a boss. Assist them in developing any new skills needed to perform competently. Call them by name, ask about their family, say thank you when they demonstrate the right attitude and effort.

"And walk in love, as Christ also hath loved us, and hath given Himself for us an offering and a sacrifice to God for a sweetsmelling savour." (Ephesians 5:2)

One little act of kindness can have multiple results. To "walk in love" means that we continually do the little acts of kindness that can make life bearable and better for another person.

> *The goal of life is to find out God's will and to do it.*

POWERFUL INFLUENCE:

YOUR LIFE EITHER SHEDS LIGHT OR CASTS A SHADOW

The way we live affects others for good or for bad. This is a sobering and challenging truth that should influence the way we, as Christians, walk and talk. It's surprising how many people go through life without ever recognizing that their feelings toward other people are largely determined by their feeling toward themselves. And, if you're not comfortable within yourself, you can't be comfortable with others—Sidney Harris

In her first twelve months in office, Indonesia's Megawati Sukarnoputri brought two rare qualities to the presidential palace: *peace and quiet.* What a transition from the former leadership. Mrs. Sukarnoputri said little in public since her election in July 2001, avoiding the outbursts of her predecessor, the blind cleric Abdurrahman Wahid, who often sent the country's currency markets into turmoil. The equity markets seem to be thanking her. Indonesia is the world's fourth most populous country, but has a relatively small stock exchange, with a capitalization of just $36 billion. The sense of relative calm in Jakarta has helped to reassure consumers and share prices have risen as demand has fueled economic growth. Private consumption rose 9.2 percent in real terms during the second half of 2001.[32]

The largest gathering of world leaders—more than 150—in history—took place on Wednesday, September 5, 2002, to chart the course of the United Nations in the 21st century, particularly its efforts to forge peace. It opened with a call for peace and an end to war. As the meeting began, it was clouded by the killings of three United Nations workers in West Timor. Former U.S. President William J. Clinton stated that he was "deeply saddened" to learn of the three murders and that The United Nations must be prepared to

---

[32] *Financial Times Newspaper*, "IndonesianThrives on Peace and Quiet," July 8, 2002, by Tom McCawley, pg. 17.

confront such hostilities. He specifically called on the Indonesian authorities "to put a stop to these abuses," as former President Abdurrahmam Wahid was in the audience. At the urging of United Nations' Secretary General Kofi Annan, the leaders held a minute of silence at the start of the meeting to commemorate the deaths of the three aid workers slain after an angry Indonesian mob and militiamen attacked and burned the office of The United Nations High Commissioner for Refugees.

In an article entitled, "World Leaders Meet for Millennium Summit," at the conclusion of the summit, world leaders were expected to adopt a so-called Millennium Declaration, which commits to eradicate poverty, promote education, and reverse the spread of HIV/AIDS. Noting that more than five million people have lost their lives in wars during the past decade, the document says, "We will spare no effort to free our peoples from the scourge of war." The nine-page draft vows to promote democracy and strengthen respect for human rights and fundamental freedoms, including "the right to development"—a key demand by Third World countries.[33]

"In whom the god of this world hath blinded the minds of them which believe not, lest the light of the glorious Gospel of Christ, who is the image of God, should shine unto them. For we preach not ourselves, but Christ Jesus the Lord, and ourselves your servants for Jesus' sake. For God, who commanded the light to shine out of darkness, hath shined in our hearts, to give the light of the knowledge of the glory of God in the face of Jesus Christ. But we have this treasure in earthen vessels, that the excellency of the power may be of God, and not of us." (2 Corinthians 4:4-7)

We cannot hide The Gospel.

---

[33] USA Today.com, September 5, 2002.

"That ye may be blameless and harmless, the sons of God,
without rebuke, in the midst of a crooked and perverse nation,
*among whom ye shine as **lights** in the world."* (Philippians 2:15)

Great men are little men expanded. Great lives are ordinary lives intensified. The Apostle Paul gives us a natural example of advancing through adversity. Because Paul was forced to spend all but seven years of his ministry in prison, we get to read his life-changing epistles, 2000 years later. A man gifted with compassion and encouragement, he authored thirteen New Testament books of *The Holy Bible* with strong and effective messages:

Paul's Letters to the Churches:

Romans—Considered Paul's greatest work, he explores the significance of Jesus' sacrificial death. Behavior must be built upon belief. It does not determine the blessing. Instead, the blessing should determine the behavior.

1 Corinthians—Application of Christian principles to carnality within the individual and in the church. Corinth was a hub of commerce, degraded culture and idolatrous religion.

2 Corinthians—Paul defends his apostolic credentials and authority. Most have repented and some have not.

Galatians—*The Christian's 'Declaration of Independence,'* blessing comes from God on the basis of faith, not law.

Ephesians—Addressed to a group of believers who are rich beyond measure in Jesus, yet who are living as beggars. "In Christ" appears about 35 times, more than in any other New Testament book.

Philippians—Only in Christ are real unity and joy possible. Paul writes a thank-you note to the believers at Philippi for their help in his hour of need.

Colossians—Perhaps the most Christ-centered book in the Bible. Focuses on the Head (Christ). Its purpose is to show that Christ is preeminent.

1 Thessalonians—Christ is seen as the believer's hope of salvation, now and at His coming. Steadfastness in The Lord is key.

2 Thessalonians—Paul deals with a misunderstanding spawned by false teachers regarding the coming day of The Lord. The major concept is the return of Christ (mentioned 318 times in The New Testament).

Letters to Individuals:

1 Timothy—Paul warns young Timothy to be a guard to avoid false teachers and greedy motives. Timothy was to organize and oversee the Asian churches as a faithful minister of God. By now, Christianity was illegal.

2 Timothy—Writing from Roman prison, Paul writes a letter of encouragement.

Titus—Titus served as Paul's special apostolic delegate to Corinth. Paul traveled with Timothy and Titus. He left Timothy in Ephesus and traveled on to Crete with Titus. He left Titus in Crete to provide leadership for the church there. In this short epistle to Titus, Paul wrote directions similar to those he had written in his first letter to Timothy. The difference is one of emphasis. In First Timothy, Paul's emphasis is on the leadership of the local church. In Titus, the emphasis is on the organization of the local church.

Philemon—In this one page Book, Paul writes a postcard about a master-slave relationship. Philemon forgives his runaway slave Onesimus for running away, after he receives Christ.

Encourage and inspire someone today. Help them to reach their potential through your zeal, passion, and love of life! Be the leader that God has called you to be and serve someone else through your gift as God has pre-ordained before the foundation of the world. Share God's plan to prosper them through the plan that He has for their life (Jeremiah 29:11).

FOOD FOR THOUGHT FOR EFFECTIVE LEADERSHIP

*A leader is one who knows the way, goes the way,
and shows the way.*

**The Ten 'Sacred Bulls' that Create Obstacles
to Your Progress at Work are The Bulls of:**

1. **Denial:** I don't see the problem, so it isn't there.

2. **Blind spots and Shortcuts:** What I don't like can't be important.

3. **Self-Interest:** Always look out for number one.

4. **Mind Reading:** People should know what I want without being told.

5. **Blame:** If something goes wrong, it has to be somebody's fault.

6. **Being Nice:** Avoid conflict at all times.

7. **Perfection:** If it's not perfect, it's nothing.

8. **Fairness:** I don't need to negotiate for what I want; I just want fairness.

9. **Excuses:** There's always a good reason why I don't follow the rules everyone else works by.

10. **Being Right:** There's a right way and a wrong way; my way is right.

Chief Executive Officer

Politician

News Reporter

Government Official

Vice President, Finance

Pastor

Administrator

Doctor

Chef

PART III

The Mentoring Years...
Raising Others' Productivity Level

"Let your **light** *so shine before men, that they may see your good works, and glorify your Father which is in heaven."*
(Matthew 5:16)

*A*s mentors, we have a responsibility to raise the level of productivity of others who are within our sphere of influence—through *excellence*. Beginning with self, we must have determination and zeal to see others excel and to become what God has called them to be. In Genesis, chapter one, verse 28, God gives four specific instructions after creating man in His image and in His likeness: *"...Be fruitful, and multiply, and replenish the earth, and subdue it."* The meaning of 'multiply' includes to raise the level of productivity of others.

Likewise, Jesus taught a multitude of followers and His disciples, during His first public sermon—The Sermon on the Mount—*"Let your **light** so shine before men, that they may see your good works, and glorify your Father which is in heaven."* (Matthew 5:16) Our *light* exposes sin, extends brightness, projects, shines, radiates, and illuminates. Why this teaching and why at this time during His public ministry? Simply, it was time for Jesus to teach throughout all of Galilee, to preach The Gospel of the kingdom, and to heal all manner of sickness and disease among the people (Matthew 4:23). It was vital at this time in history that men see His *good works* so that God be glorified in heaven.

First, be an inspiration—something that people can see and aspire to become. The life of Dr. Martin Luther King, Jr., is a true inspiration to millions. Secondly, walk by faith and not by sight (2 Corinthians 5:7). Trust in God and not the circumstances or situations at work. Change is a constant and consistent reality in this world, but God never changes. Thirdly, be a great communicator and explain what you mean. Effective communication does not take place until the recipient of your message hears, receives, and acknowledges the message. A confirmation of understanding is necessary. Poor communication is perhaps the biggest challenge facing the workplace today, especially in corporate America. There is too much emphasis on achieving results—whether clearly understood or not—with little or no direction, guidance, nor proper roadmap to assist in delivering the expected outcome or results. Misconceptions, misinterpretations, and misunderstandings are the direct result of poor communication. Evangelist Billy Graham is a great communicator as evidenced by the thousands, perhaps millions, of people who have confessed Jesus Christ as their personal Lord and Savior over the fifty years that he has preached The Gospel. Crusade after crusade, year after year, Rev. Graham effectively communicated the comforting message that "God loves you and He gave His only begotten Son for you. Come to Jesus…"

Chapter Seven

Be an Inspiration, Not an Obstacle

"I have an inner urge calling me to serve humanity."
—Rev. Dr. Martin Luther King, Jr.
Remarks prior to his ordination as a minister at the age of 19

"This then is the message which we have heard of Him, and declare unto you, that God is light, *and in Him is no darkness at all. If we say that we have fellowship with Him, and walk in darkness, we lie, and do not the truth: but if we walk in the* light, *as He is in the* light, *we have fellowship one with another, and the blood of Jesus Christ His Son cleanseth us from all sin."* (1 John 1:5-7)

Inspire others to excel through your character, work ethic, and integrity.

*I*n the Book of Genesis, chapter one, God reveals unto Adam that he is blessed and to be fruitful, multiply, replenish the earth, and subdue it. God's specific instructions are to be *productive, raise the level of productivity of those around us, leave a deposit in the earth for the next generation,* and *to control our environment.* What an awesome responsibility that God entrusts us with! It takes inspiration to be a productive person and to raise others' level of productivity because our actions inspire them to do so.

Rev. Dr. Martin Luther King, Jr. is one of the world's greatest inspirations. He truly inspired all Americans to change an entire culture, custom, practice, and mindset—discrimination based upon skin color. Dr. King is the only American-born citizen who has a birthday designated as a holiday in his name. He defined greatness through the service that he tirelessly rendered. From 1955 to 1968, he led peaceful demonstrations against evil throughout the United States, particularly in the south. He inspired millions to follow his peaceful demonstrations. This was partly because of his stance on not being afraid to die for a cause that is just, right, fair, equitable, and scriptural. Tapped as one of the most important speeches in the 20th century, Dr. King's *'I Have A Dream'* is replayed every year as America celebrates the life and legacy of this great servant of The Lord on his birthday, January fifteenth.

Having skipped two grades in high school, Dr. King began college at the tender age of fifteen. He was such an inspirational leader that he led a 381-day bus boycott in Montgomery, Alabama in response to Rosa Parks' refusal to needlessly abandon her seat. During the

1950's, the state law stipulated that she had to surrender her seat to a white person, even if other seats are available. This law made no sense, but the courage to challenge this was lacking. God shows love to all people and is no respecter of persons (James 2:9), and finally, under leadership, the state of Alabama's decision to arbitrarily defy God's Word was ignored. Dr. King declared, *"It is better to walk in humility than to ride in humiliation."* It was a spark that caught thousands on fire and caused them to take an active role in bankrupting a corrupt state government system. However, his compassion was equally comforting when he said that through nonviolent and peaceful protests, *"We can turn any man into a friend."*

Dr. King was so focused on his calling to be an inspirational leader that he only granted one television interview. This was granted to Arnold McCalah. Yet, he was arrested thirty times for taking a stand for justice, righteousness, equity, and fair treatment for all people. On the eve of his assassination, April 3, 1968, Dr. King delivered his infamous *'I've Been to the Mountaintop'* speech. It was a night in which he was sick and had sent Dr. Ralph Abernathy to speak in his absence. Instead, he arrived and delivered an inspirational address that is replayed every year for us to remember as one of his most powerful. He described his mountaintop experience as if he knew that April 4, 1968 would be his last day as an earthen vessel for The Lord. Most notably, at Dr. King's homegoing service, one of his sermons was played and he specifically requested that no one boast about his life. Instead, he requested that we remember him in the following way:

- He tried to give his life serving others.

- He tried to love somebody.

- Remember him as a drum major for justice.

- Don't mention his awards or his Nobel Peace Prize.

More than 35 years after his assassination, He remains a model for all pastors. His impact on the church, particularly the African-American church, and the community it serves, remains the standard against which all preachers are measured. The chronology of Dr. King's life is detailed and impressive, but several accomplishments that changed America during his lifetime are worth noting:

1947	Licensed to preach and begins assisting his father, who is Pastor of Ebenezer Baptist Church in Atlanta.
1951	Graduates from Crozer with Bachelor of Divinity Degree. He is the class valedictorian and winner of the Pearl Plafker Award for most outstanding student. He begins doctoral studies in Theology at Boston University.
1956	
June 4	U.S. District Court rules racial segregation on Alabama's city bus lines is unconstitutional.
1957	
September 9	Congress passes the 1957 Civil Rights Act, first civil rights legislation since Reconstruction.
1959	
February	Dr. and Mrs. King travel to India as guests of Prime Minister Nehru to study Gandhi's techniques of nonviolence.
1960	
May 6	The 1960 Civil Rights Act is signed.
December	U.S. Supreme Court declares discrimination in bus terminal restaurants operated for the service of interstate passengers is a violation of the Interstate Commerce Act.

1961

November   Interstate Commerce Commission bans segregation on buses, trains, and supportive facilities.

1964

January 3   *Time* Magazine names Dr. King Man of the Year.

1964

July 2   Witnesses the signing of the 1964 Civil Rights Act by President Lyndon Johnson—the most far-reaching civil rights legislation since Reconstruction.

1964

December 10   Awarded the Nobel Peace Prize in Oslo, Norway—the youngest person to win the prize.

1965

August 6   President Johnson signs the 1965 Voting Rights Act.

1967

November 7   Carl Stokes elected Mayor of Cleveland, Ohio, the first Black elected mayor of a major U.S. city.

1968

April 4   Dr. King assassinated at Lorraine Motel.

April 7   The President declares a national day of mourning for King.

1986   First National King Holiday celebrated.

"Our lives begin to end the day we become silent about things that matter." [34]

---

[34] Dr. Martin Luther King, Jr.

"Let freedom ring!" are the concluding words from perhaps the most memorable speech in the history of the United States of America: *"Let freedom ring from the mighty mountains of New York...the heightening Alleghenies of Pennsylvania...the snowcapped Rockies of Colorado...the curvaceous slopes of California...*But not only that...*from Stone Mountain of Georgia...from Lookout Mountain of Tennessee...from every hill and molehill of Mississippi...*from every mountainside, *let freedom ring."* —*I Have A Dream*, Martin Luther King, Jr., pages 29-31, 1993, Anniversary Edition.

"New issues have emerged as a result of rapid technological development, such as the fight to preserve the environment, and a woman's right to reproductive choice. These are being addressed all over the U.S. by non-violent protest, inspired by Dr. King's message. It is my conviction that as new technologies emerge, they often bring tradition into conflict with new values. The tools Dr. King has given us, will enable us to confront each new issue as it arises. The struggles may change, but the tools remain constant, and for that we are indebted."[35]

'INSPIRATION' DEFINED

Inspiration, in the Greek, is translated as *Theopneustos* and means "inspired by God." It comes from two words – *Theos* (God) and *Pneō* (to breathe). The Scripture that best describes this word is found in 2 Timothy 3:16, which states:

"All scripture is given by inspiration of God, and is profitable for doctrine, for reproof, for correction, for instruction in righteousness." (2 Timothy 3:16)

Inspiration of God describes the unique character of Scripture. (1) It's not only written by men, but authored by God. (2) "For doctrine" means to tell one what to believe. (3) "For reproof"

---

[35] "A Remembrance of Dr. Martin Luther King, Jr.," by Benedict J. Fernandez— www.kodak.com, January 15, 2001

means to tell one what is wrong. (4) "For correction" means to tell one how to correct wrong. (5) "For instruction in righteousness" means to tell one how to live.

Why?

> *"That the man of God may be perfect, thoroughly furnished unto all good works."* (2 Timothy 3:17)

"Perfect" (proficient or capable) means having everything needed to do what God wants. "Thoroughly furnished" means equipped. God's inspired Word, properly used and applied, provides all that we need for life and ministry.

> *"Everywhere I go, I find that people—both leaders and individuals—are asking one basic question: 'Is there any hope for the future? Is there any hope for peace, justice, and prosperity in our generation?"* —Billy Graham

---

> *If you have a job without aggravations, you don't have a job.* —Malcomb Forbes

---

ANY DEFINITION OF A SUCCESSFUL LIFE MUST INCLUDE SERVING OTHERS

Serve Man

There are high spots in all of our lives, and most of them have come about through encouragement from someone else. I don't care how great, how famous, or successful a man or woman may be, each hungers for applause. —George Adams

The deepest principle in human nature is the craving to be appreciated.

> *"But he that is greatest among you shall be your servant."* (Matthew 23:11)

As Jesus denounces the customs, practices, philosophies, hypocrisies, and traditions of the Pharisees and the scribes, He teaches us that to be a servant means to be a 'minister' or 'attendant.' That is the true meaning of the word.

We are to serve others with the gift that God has freely given to us. The word "gift" is defined as *"Drea"* in The New Testament and denotes a "free gift," stressing its gratuitous character. In The New Testament, it is always used in reference to a spiritual or supernatural gift. Examples include John 4:10, Acts 8:20 and 11:17, Romans 5:15, 2 Corinthians 9:15, Ephesians 3:7, and Hebrews 6:4. In Ephesians 4:7, *"According to the measure of the gift of Christ,"* the "gift" is that given by Christ. In Acts 2:28, *"the gift of the Holy Ghost,"* makes the clause epexegetical, the "gift" is The Holy Ghost himself.

A free gift that is never taken away by God, it is either used or remains dormant as it relates to glorifying God. According to His Word, we are responsible and accountable for our gifts and to fulfill our purpose for being birthed into the earth. *"For the gifts and calling of God are without repentance."* (Romans 11:29)

Through the will (choice) of man, Romans 12:6-8 identifies the seven functional gifts that specifically identify our responsibilities toward society and one another in the body of Christ. How we are to conduct our everyday affairs in the presence of people who have no relationship with God (verse 20), as well as the brothers and sisters in Christ (verse 13), is taught in this scripture. The functional gifts are:

Prophesy (encouragement by the measure of faith),

Ministry (service with patience),

Exhortation (wise counsel),

Teaching (instruction),

Giving (giving without complication; simplicity is key),

Ruling (diligent leadership), and

Showing mercy (cheerful compassion).

Gift *(Hebrew or Greek word)* Original meaning in Hebrew or Greek

Prophesy *(prophēteia)*—speaking forth the mind and counsel of God. The declaration of that which cannot be known by natural means (the foretelling of the will of God whether with reference to past, present, or future).

Ministry *(diakonia)*—service; servant of The Lord in preaching and teaching.

Exhortation *(paraklēsis)*—a calling to one's side; to one's aid; consolidation and comfort.

Teaching *(didaskalia)*—that which is taught; doctrine; instruction; learning. Occurs 15 times in The New Testament.

Giving *(charizomai)*—"to show favor or kindness"; to give freely, bestow graciously. Refers mostly to what is "given" by God.

Ruling *(proistēmi)*—to stand before, to lead, attend to (indicating care and diligence). Is translated "to rule" (middle voice), with reference to a local church.

Showing mercy *(eleos)*—the outward manifestation of pity.

Upon further examination of the 12th chapter of Romans, The Apostle Paul instructs us on proper responsibilities toward the society in general. Beginning in verse 3, he reminds us that through the grace that has been given by God, we are to be humble and not to think too highly of ourselves. This is applicable to all situations and circumstances in life. As God has dealt to all men, and women, the measure of faith, we are commanded to exercise our gift(s) with humility and in faith. Paul's purpose for this instruction is so that we would be mindful that each of the seven functional spiritual gifts have a different benefit within the body of Christ, yet we are one body in Christ and each of us are members one of another (verses 4—6). As we *function together* as one, in love, which is the overriding theme, it becomes less challenging to apply God's Word to our daily lives. In verses 9-21, we are specifically instructed to love, serve, extend kindness, be instant in prayer, be honest, serve The Lord, overcome evil with good, live peaceably with all men, and not seek revenge. These instructions apply to all situations and to all of God's people. The blessings of God's functional gift(s) allow us to remain in obedience to His Word. Circumstances and situations shall not prevail, but The Word of God shall prevail in our life!

If a man's gift is encouraging, let him encourage. If a man's gift is ministry, let him serve with patience. If a man's gift is ruling, let him do so through diligent leadership. If a man's gift is teaching, let him instruct. If a man's gift is exhortation, let him do so through wise counsel. If a man loves to give, let him give without complicating matters. If a man's gift is showing mercy, let him be cheerful in doing so.

> *"Having then gifts differing according to the grace that*
> *is given to us..."* (Romans 12:6)

Serve God

To *"glorify"* means to praise and worship (Psalm 86:9). It means to admire, point out the good in, and recognize as glorious. A Christian's greatest calling is to glorify God through his or her actions, words, and character (Matthew 5:16). Christians glorify God by obeying Him and living His way. Specific examples include sexual purity (1 Corinthians 6:20), choosing the right words (1Peter 4:11), living as a Christian (Romans 15:6), and imitating Jesus (John 17:10-11). As Christians, we are followers of Jesus Christ (Acts 11:26 and 26:28; 1 Peter 4:16). Ones who belong to Christ, Christians commit themselves to Christ and become increasingly like Him. We trust Jesus Christ to guide our decisions, actions, and attitudes. To handle yourself, use your head; To handle others, use your heart.

> *"This then is the message which we have heard of him, and*
> *declare unto you, that God is light, and in Him is no darkness at*
> *all. If we say that we have fellowship with Him, and walk in*

darkness, we lie, and do not the truth: But if we walk in the light, as He is in the light, we have fellowship one with another, and the blood of Jesus Christ His Son cleanseth us from all sin."
(1 John 1:5-7)

God is perfect and good. There is no sin or evil in Him. This has implications for followers of Him as we look to Him as our Heavenly Father. (1) "Walk in darkness" means to walk in sin. If we walk in darkness, we cannot enjoy a close relationship with God. (2) To "walk in His light," which means to live free from the bondage of sin, makes true communion between believers possible. (3) The blood of Jesus represents the cleansing and ultimate defense against sin's presence and power.

"And it came to pass, as they still went on, and talked, that, behold, there appeared a chariot of fire, and horses of fire, and parted them both asunder; and Elijah went up by a whirlwind into heaven." (2 Kings 2:11)

Elijah followed Enoch in being taken into heaven without dying. This parallels Genesis 5:24, which states: "And Enoch walked with God: and he was not; for God took him."

Elijah was a well-loved prophet of Israel who took a stand for God against false religious leaders and kings (1 Kings 17:1; 18; 21:17-29). He is best known for discrediting Baal and Baal's prophets on Mount Carmel and for hearing a still, small voice (1Kings 18; 19:12-13). Rather than dying, Elijah was taken up into heaven in a whirlwind. John the Baptist was sometimes referred to as Elijah. Elijah appeared to Jesus on the Mount of Transfiguration and his name means Yahweh is God. He was succeeded by Elisha.

BE PREPARED TO INSPIRE!

During your lifetime, you will directly or indirectly influence the lives of 10,000 other people. How will you influence them? Demetrius, for example, is well spoken of by everyone and even by the truth itself. He was a Christian commended for his witness. *"Demetrius hath good report of all men, and of the truth itself: yea, and we also bear record; and ye know that our record is true."* (3 John 12)

Prepare for the day that your mentor will not be around (Joshua-Moses; Paul-Timothy; Elijah-Elisha; David-Solomon). God is always preparing someone to carry out His work and to take it to the next level. Do not allow someone that you can influence to be untrained or unlearned as they progress to the next level. Do not evade them or leave them with questions, getting caught in scams, orchestrating unscrupulous business practices, or participating in unrighteousness. Make a difference in the life of another person and do it now!

"I believe I evaded that question earlier."

©2003; Reprinted courtesy of Bunny Hoest and Parade.

Inspire in the midst of the distractions

Several polls indicate that there are five primary office distractions. They are:

1. Chatting

2. Personal phone calls

3. Electronic noises (computer, cell phones, pagers)

4. Air quality

5. Lighting[36]

In the midst of these top five distractions, there are six primary types of disruptive workers to contend with at the office. Disruptive co-workers fall into the following categories with a brief description of each:

The Chatterbox—Talkative, ignorant, selfish, irritating, unaware of others, disrespectful, uncommunicative and boring. They are talkaholics.

The Competitor—Provocative, fearless, paranoid, offensive, pushy, aggressive, resentful, confrontational, and sabotaging. Always looking for a fight.

The Gossip—Indiscreet, insecure, fault-finding, competitive, hurtful, self-righteous, offensive and angry.

The Jokester—Annoying, insecure, weak, obnoxious, selfish, corny, offensive, superficial, desperate for attention, and unaware of others.

The Cut-You-Downer—Arrogant, mean, belittling, hateful, self-righteous, condescending, threatening, insecure, underhanded, and fault-finding.

---

[36] American Society of Interior Designers; Stephen Viscusi, author of *On the Job—How to Make It in the Real World of Work.*

The Gloom-and-Doom Victim—Masochistic, guilt-ridden, worrisome, sabotaging, resentful, rigid, selfish, sad, negative, petty, lackadaisical and defensive.[37]

Let us live that when we die, even the undertaker will be sorry. You can preach a better sermon with your life than with your lips. As God gave us His Word through inspiration, inspire others, despite their faults, through the Word of God. Lead by example. Inspire others to excel through your character, work ethic, and integrity. Be an inspiration, not an obstacle.

---

[37] "How to Handle Disruptive Co-Workers," by Lisa Irizarry, *The Star-Ledger* staff, May 26, 2002, page 2, Section Two.

FOOD FOR THOUGHT

FOR AVOIDING OBSTACLES

Following the path of least resistance is what makes
rivers—and people—crooked.

Chapter Eight

Walk By Faith, Not By Sight

"For we walk by faith, not by sight!"
—Dr. Frederick K.C. Price, Pastor, Crenshaw Christian Center, Los Angeles, California, as he concludes his weekly Ever Increasing Faith Ministries sermons broadcast on over 115 television stations worldwide

"For we walk by faith, not by sight …."
—**2 Corinthians 5:7**

**Despite constant change, obstacles,
and disappointments, walk by faith.**

*H*ow you think about a problem is more important than the problem itself. So always think positively. We are made up of three parts—soul (our will, thoughts and emotions), body (our means of survival on earth through the five sensory perceptions—taste, smell, sight, touch, and hearing), and spirit (the 'real' you—how we make contact with God The Almighty). The inner man, spirit, is made alive when we confess Jesus Christ as our personal Lord and Savior—the prayer of salvation. We then enter into The Faith of Jesus, who is the author and finisher of our Faith (Hebrews 12:2). As an heir to the inheritance of Our Heavenly Father, and co-heir with Jesus Christ, we can and should walk by faith and not by sight.

We are bombarded daily by visual stimulation—things we see—that influence our actions, thoughts, and words. We are, however, on an assignment in the earth, as ambassadors for Christ, to fulfill God's plan for our lives. Better yet, we already have victory through God's Word.

"But thanks be to God, which giveth us the victory through Our Lord Jesus Christ." (1 Corinthians 15:57)

> *I don't know the key to success, but the key to failure is trying to please everybody.* —*Bill Cosby*

When Dave Thomas died in early 2002, he left behind more than just thousands of Wendy's Restaurants. He also left a legacy of being a practical, hard-working man who was respected for his down-to-earth values.

Among the pieces of good advice that have outlived the smiling entrepreneur is his view of what Christians should be doing with their lives. In his book entitled, *Well Done*, Thomas said, "Roll-up-your-shirtsleeve Christians and see Christianity as faith and action. They still make the time to talk with God through prayer, study Scripture with devotion, be super-active in their church, and take their ministry to others to spread the Good Word." He went on to say they are "anonymous people who may be doing even more good than all the well-known Christians in the world."

A living faith is a working faith (James 2:18).

MANAGEMENT STYLE FADS COME AND GO

Over the past century, businesses have embraced many different management strategies. Some have been inspired by science more than by art. Today's workplace is a mosaic of them:

1908—Model T's begin assembly line. Henry Ford's scientific method revolutionizes the manufacturing process.

1923—Alfred Sloan takes the helm at General Motors. His genius for marketing and organization at the company pushes him to the forefront of leading management practices.

1956—William Whyte's book *The Organization Man* criticizes the sterile bureaucracy of American business and calls for im mediate change.

1960—*The Human Side of Enterprise* by Douglas McGregor introduces a new concept: Business with a human face. Employees and customers benefit.

1963—Boston Consulting Group is founded, beginning the rise and influence of professional management consultants.

1982—*In Search of Excellence,* by two McKinsey consultants, touches off a craze of management books and fads that American firms glom onto in search of answers. *The One Minute Manager* becomes a big seller.

1993—Business process re-engineering emerges during lean times. It translates into mass layoffs at many companies.

1995—The Internet era begins. Information workers emerge as do stock options, lattes, and office toys galore! This nonsense does not last long.

2003—AOL Time Warner embraces a low-key Chief Executive Officer and a back-to-basics approach.

I will take God's Word over any and all of man's management fads any day. In the introduction of this book, I demonstrated through God's Word that He does not change. There is tremendous comfort in knowing that we serve a God that cannot, and will not, change. His Word is His bond! In His presence, I can do all things and be all that God has called me to be.

"Thou shall hide them in the secret of thy presence from the pride of man: thou shalt keep them secretly in a pavilion from the strife of tongues." (Psalm 31:20)

In the shelter of His presence, He hides us.

There are six comforting things that you will find in God's presence that you will not find anywhere else:

Hope—Psalm 118:13/21:
"Thou hast thrust sore at me that I might fall:
but the LORD helped me"
"I will praise thee: for thou hast heard me,
and art become my salvation."

Love—Romans 5:5:

"And hope maketh not ashamed; because the love of God is shed abroad in our hearts by The Holy Ghost which is given unto us."

Protection—Psalm 31:20-21:

"Thou shalt hide them in the secret of thy presence from the pride of man: thou shalt keep them secretly in a pavilion from the strife of tongues. Blessed be the LORD for He hath shewed me His marvelous kindness in a strong city."

Forgiveness—Isaiah 1:18:

"Come now, and let us reason together, saith The LORD: though your sins be as scarlet, they shall be as white as snow; though they be red like crimson, they shall be as wool."

Direction—Isaiah 30:21:

"And thine ears shall hear a word behind thee, saying, This is the way, walk ye in it, when ye turn to the right hand, and when ye turn to the left."

Joy—Psalm 16:11 and John 16:24:

"Thou wilt shew me the path of life: in thy presence is fullness of joy; at thy right hand there are pleasures for evermore."

Your alternative is to trust in man, who changes frequently and ultimately abandons that plan and direction for the organization or company. It is abandoned because it did not work out as planned. Do not follow the scientific mind of man as he tries to figure out what God already knows. God commands us to love Him, hate sin, and to give freely unto men—giving of your resources, energy, knowledge, and time unto your fellow man and woman.

TRAFFIC, EVERYONE KNOWS, IS ONE OF THE BIGGER HASSLES OF MODERN LIFE

Walking by faith and not by sight can be a challenge during the typical commute to the office. Remember to focus on what God will have you to do rather than the circumstances surrounding that assignment. In an article entitled, "American Gridlock," by Phillip J. Longman, *U.S. News and World Report,* May 28, 2001, it was reported that 'traffic is making millions sick and tired. The bad news? It's going to get worse unless things change in a real big way.'

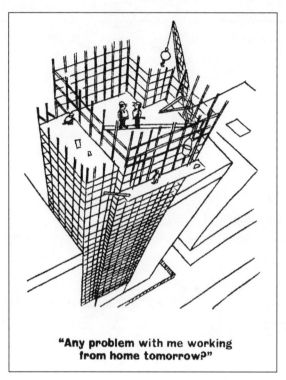

"Any problem with me working from home tomorrow?"

© 2003; Reprinted courtesy of Bunny Hoest and Parade.

The advent of suburbia after the end of World War II led to a wave of commuters traveling into the big cities for office jobs. Since 1982, while the U.S. population has grown nearly 20 percent, the time Americans spend in traffic has jumped an amazing 236 percent. In major American cities, the length of the combined morning-evening rush hour has doubled, from under three hours in 1982 to almost six hours today. The result? The average driver now spends the equivalent of nearly a full workweek each year stuck in traffic.

That's not just lost time, but it's real money. Congestion costs Americans $78 billion per year in wasted fuel and lost time. That's an increase of 39 percent since 1990. In New Jersey's Somerset county, where I reside, congestion costs the average licensed driver $2,100 a year. Further, I have personally experienced the dreadful two-hour door-to-door commute into midtown Manhattan. On occasion, the commute has been three hours—one way!

> *Congestion costs Americans nearly $80 billion a year in wasted time and fuel. Never mind the aggravation—UGGHHH!*

According to the most recent federal data, the amount of time mothers spend behind the wheel increased by eleven percent just between 1990 and 1995, and there's every indication that the trend is continuing. Moms spend more time driving than they spend dressing, bathing, and feeding a child. Indicative of the growing concern about traffic among social conservatives, The Washington Family Council concludes in a report: "The long-term consequences of traffic reach far beyond simple economics; it seeps into the foundation of society—people and their families." It is reported that a clinical psychologist in Stockton, CA, just outside of San Francisco, counsels 12 to 15 married couples each week, about half of which struggle with commuter-related stress. According to the psychologist, "They come in quarreling too much, the affection's gone, and so is the sex. They have only a dim awareness that commuting is the problem."

Stressed-out commuters with little time for loved ones also don't have time for community involvement. Robert Putnam, professor of public policy at Harvard University, has conducted extensive studies of reasons behind Americans' decreasing involvement in social groups like the Parent-Teachers Association, church, recreational clubs, and political parties. Putnam's conclusion? Long commutes are a bigger reason than almost any demographic factor. This relationship can be plotted on a curve, Putnam says: For every ten minutes spent driving to work, involvement in community affairs drops by ten percent. Annual delay/drop per person, in hours:

Hours	City
56	Los Angeles
53	Seattle
50	Houston
46	Washington, DC
45	Austin, Denver
44	St. Louis
42	San Francisco, Orlando, Miami, Boston, Nashville
41	Detroit
38	Minneapolis-St. Paul
34	Chicago, New York, Portland
33	Albuquerque
32	Charlotte
31	Phoenix[38]

WHAT IS YOUR MOUNTAIN EXPERIENCE?

Mount Everest is the gold medal in the Olympic Games of mountaineering. At 29,028 feet, it is the tallest mountain in the world and represents the highest point of achievement for humans on the face of the earth. Sitting astride the border between Tibet to the north and Nepal to the south, Everest is a huge mass of black, forbidding rock and ice that dominates the landscape in every direction.

Meet Mr. John Amatt, a member of the first Canadian expedition to reach the summit of Mount Everest. In the introduction of his

---

[38] Texas Transportation Institute—Texas A&M University

book entitled, ***Straight to the Top and Beyond—Nine Keys for Meeting the Challenge of Changing Times***, ©1995, he encourages his readers with the following quote:

> *The challenge of change is forcing us to rethink our values and to rekindle the spirit of adventure. It will take courage, resourcefulness and endurance to meet this challenge—the courage to try, to commit and to take risks; the resourcefulness to be innovative and creative in finding new ways of doing old things; and the endurance to keep going when the going gets tough.*

> *It is one of the great paradoxes of human existence that, by nature, we seek out comfort and predictability, using all of our financial resources and intellectual powers to devise technologies that will make our lives easier and less stressful. The paradox is that once we have created the comfort we desire, we must leave it all behind if we are to move forward toward future opportunity.*

His parents, on their honeymoon in 1936, climbed in the Bernese Alps of Switzerland and, two years later, reached the summit of the 12,142-foot Wetterhorn, a mountain that his sister and he climbed when he was 18 years old.

Also, in 1938, his parents were present in Grindlewald when the deadly north face of the Eiger was climbed for the first time, at that point, it was the most dramatic climb in history.

In chapter ten of his book, Mr. Amatt introduces a faith principle that he calls: *Adventure Attitude*. The nine keys of T*he Adventure Attitude* are:

A: Adaptability
Change is not merely necessary to life. It is life! By the same token, life in adaptation. —Alvin Toffler

D: Desire and Determination

You've got to hang on to your dreams. Great dreams don't happen overnight.

V: Vision and Values

Vision...is the ability to:
Look to the past and learn from it;
Look to the present and be attuned to it;
Look to the future and be prepared for it.
—Unknown

E: Experience

The only failure in life is when we fail to learn the lessons from our experience.

N: Natural Curiosity

If we're not pushing our limits, we're not discovering anything new.

T: Teamwork and Trust

Rarely do we achieve complete success in today's changing world without the help and support of others. The essence of teamwork is to identify and use the strengths of others to offset our own limitations, so that the strength of the team becomes greater than the sum of the individual parts.

U: Unlimited Optimism

Life is a leap of faith. There is no way that we can know what will happen tomorrow.

R: Risk-ability

The only limiting factor to our achievements in life is our fear of the unknown.

E: Exceptional Performance

Achievement is the constant process of going one step beyond your previous experience.

"The thief cometh not, but for to steal, to kill, and to destroy: I am come that they might have life, and that they might have it more abundantly." (John 10:10)

As the mountain climber gets an occasional exhilaration from climbing, we get the most out of life when we live for Christ. I see a wholehearted application of the Christian's experience. Jesus did not call us to live the Christian life merely to escape hell. It's not a life of minimum joy and fulfillment, but a life that is full and overflowing. Our purpose in following Christ should not be merely to avoid eternal punishment. If that is our primary motivation, we are missing the wonders, joys and victories of reaching higher heights with Jesus.

Do not live minimally. Live life to the maximum. Climb that mountain with confidence!

"While we look not at the things which are seen, but at the things which are not seen: for the things which are seen are temporal; but the things which are not seen are eternal."
(2 Corinthians 4:18)

FOOD FOR THOUGHT

BELIEVING THE 'UNSEEN'

As the clock ticked over to 08:01 P.M. on Wednesday, February 20, 2002, time read (only for sixty seconds) in perfect symmetry. To be more precise: 20:02, 2002. It was an event that has only ever happened once before. The last occasion that time read in such a symmetrical pattern was long before the days of the digital watch (or the 24-hour clock): 10:10 A.M. on January 10, 1001. And because the clock only goes up to 23:59, it is something that will never happen again.

Chapter Nine

Explain What You Mean

"God loves you and He gave His only begotten Son for you. Come to Jesus..."
—Evangelist Billy Graham, as he concludes each of the local, regional, national, and international crusades with a call to Christ.

"For God hath not given us the spirit of fear, but of power, and of love, and of a sound mind." (2 Timothy 1:7)

Be a great communicator and eliminate all guesswork.

*T*he life of Evangelist Billy Graham is fascinating and phenomenal. I have listened to his sermons (rhema—the spoken word) and have read a number of his books including *Just As I Am—The Autobiography of Billy Graham* (1997), *Peace with God* (1953), *How to be Born Again* (1977), and *Billy Graham—God's Ambassador* (1999). His sermons are consistent and meaningful as evidenced here:

> *"I have had the privilege of preaching The Gospel on every continent in most of the countries of the world.*
> *And I have found that when I present the simple message of The Gospel of Jesus Christ, with authority, quoting from the very Word of God—He takes that message and drives it supernaturally into the human heart."*—Billy Graham

William Franklin Graham, Jr. was born in the downstairs bedroom of a frame farmhouse on November 7, 1918, three days before his father's 30th birthday. His parents called him Billy Frank. On Easter Sunday evening, 1937, he preached his first sermon at Bostwick Baptist Church, a country church near Palatka, Florida. His sermon lasted eight minutes. Today, he is one of the most recognizable figures in the world—a man who, for more than fifty years, spoke in person to over 100 million people on six continents, in eighty-five countries, and in all of America's fifty states—more than any other man or woman in history. He has ministered to millions around the world, has counseled Presidents and Prime Ministers, and was the driving force behind the evangelical movement of the twentieth century. One of his most profound statements is: *"My one purpose in life is to help people find a personal relationship with God, which, I believe, comes through Jesus Christ."*

He is a man who consistently means what he says. God's Word says, *"And I, if I be lifted up from the earth, I will draw all men unto me."* (John 12:32). Evangelist Graham is forthright in his local, regional, national, and international crusades. He has spoken before millions of people, perhaps billions, in almost every country in the world. His sermons are:

• **Pure:**　　　　　　　Clean hands and a pure heart
　　　　　　　　　　　(Psalm 24:4)
*"I am convinced that the greatest act of love we can ever perform
　for people is to tell them about God's love for them in Christ."*

• **Genuine**:　　　　　Not "puffed up," but humble
　　　　　　　　　　　(1 Peter 5:6)

*"I would like to say that I am just one man among many that have
come for this crusade. We have a whole team of people and most
of us have been together for nearly fifty years. I'm introduced as
though I'm doing it all. They have far greater skills than I have,
they have far greater abilities and gifts than I have. But it's The
Lord using this group of people along with the local churches to
make Christ known to the community."*　 The largest crowd at any
event in the Los Angeles Memorial Coliseum was the 1963 Billy
Graham crusade, with 134,254 inside and 20,000 more outside.

• **Focused:**　　　　　Knows his audience
　　　　　　　　　　　(Luke 19:10)
*"I had used from 25 to 100 passages of Scripture with every
sermon and learned that modern man will surrender
to the impact of the Word of God."*

• **Christ-centered:**　Always lifts up the name of Jesus
　　　　　　　　　　　(John 12:32)
*"I present a God who matters, and who makes claims on the
human race. He is a God of love, grace, mercy, but also a God of
judgment. When we break His moral laws we suffer; when we*

keep them we have inward peace and joy. I am calling for a revival that will cause men and women to return to their offices and shops to live out the teaching of Christ in their daily relationships. I preach a Gospel not of despair but of hope for the individual, hope for society, and hope for the world."

• **Simple:**   Everyone can understand
                    (Proverbs 1:4)

"God is a God of love, a God of mercy. He has the hairs of your head numbered...He wants to come into your life and give you new hope." —In October 1974, the largest crowd to attend an evangelistic service in the Western Hemisphere—225,000 people—filled Rio de Janeiro's Maracana Stadium.

• **Fearless and direct:** An excellent communicator
                    (Romans 12:13-18)

"Nowhere in Mark 16:15— 'Go ye into all the world, and preach The Gospel to every creature'—nor in any similar Scripture—did Christ command us to go only into the western or capitalist world and nowhere did He say to exclude the Communist world."—In July 1967, Billy Graham preached for the first time inside a Communist country—Yugoslavia. Technically, it was not part of the Soviet bloc, yet these were Eastern Europe's first open-air evangelistic meetings since World War II.

• **Honest:**   Tells the truth
                    (John 8:32)

"I am convinced, through my travels and experiences, that people all over the world are hungry to hear the Word of God. As the people came to a desert place to hear John the Baptist proclaim, 'Thus saith the Lord, so modern man in his confusions, frustrations, and bewilderment will come to hear the minister who preaches with authority.'" —In March 1973, Johannesburg's Wanderers Stadium held 60,000 people, making it the largest multiracial gathering ever held in South Africa to that time.

• **Impactful:**   Bold and uncompromising
             (1 John 4:17)

"I had some hesitancy about taking this engagement because it was a variety show. However, I remembered that Jesus ate with publicans and sinners, even though He was denounced by the Pharisees. Here was an opportunity to give my testimony to 40 million Americans over NBC Television."

• **Moving:**   Sincere and passionate in his delivery
             (Matthew 5:16)

"The real story of the crusades is not in the great choirs, the thousands in attendance, nor the hundreds of inquirers who are counseled. The real story is in the changes that have taken place in the hearts and lives of people."—In June 1973, a record 1.1 million people made Yoido Plaza in Seoul, South Korea, Billy Graham's largest ever meeting held anywhere in the world.

• **Results-oriented:**   Always concludes with a call to Christ
             (Romans 10:9)

"This is the spot that thousands of tourists think of as New York. Many foreign visitors judge America by Times Square Some stare in wonderment at the blaze of lights; others hurry along streets to the theaters and places of amusement. Here in Times Square is the dope addict, the alcoholic, the harlot, along with the finest citizens of the world. Let us tell the whole world tonight we Americans believe in God!"—Closing Sermon of the New York Crusade, September 1, 1957.

"For He saith, I have heard thee in a time accepted, and in the day of salvation have I succoured thee: behold, now is the accepted time; behold, now is the day of salvation."
(2 Corinthians 6:2)

NOW is the day of salvation!

Dubbed the 'World's Most Famous Preacher,' Evangelist Billy Graham's 412th crusade took place in Dallas, Texas, before a record crowd at Texas Stadium that spilled out into an adjacent parking lot where thousands of chairs were set up beneath a giant Jumbo-Tron screen. On this October evening, the frail, white-haired, 84-year-old evangelist slowly made his way to the pulpit to deliver the same simple message he had preached to more than 210 million people in over 180 countries for more than half a century: *"God loves you and He gave His begotten Son for you. Come to Jesus..."*[39]

---

*Words to live by are just words,
unless we live by them.*

WORDS ARE POWERFUL

Man's inability to communicate effectively is a result of his failure to listen skillfully and with understanding to another person.
—Carl Rogers, psychologist.

Words, like eyeglasses, blur everything that they do not make clear. —Joseph Joubert.

Good communication is as stimulating as black coffee and just as hard to sleep after. —Anne Morrow Lindbergh

Communication is the key to success. Pass it on.

---

[39] *U.S. News and World Report,* "A Christian Dynasty, How Billy Graham's Kids are Firing Up His Crusade," page 38.

"We need a signed authorization to obtain a certificate to register for a license to apply for a permit."

©2003; Reprinted courtesy of Bunny Hoest and Parade.

Sticks & Stones...

There is a popular saying that is mentioned regularly by children, men and women of all ages. It has to do with our futile attempts to demonstrate to others that their words do not affect us—especially the unkind ones. Although this saying is well known and often quoted, it is wrong. It goes like this:

> *"Sticks and stones may break my bones,*
> *but words will never hurt me."*

Unfortunately, this is not completely true. Words can either give life or cause death. They are so powerful, that 'word' is used 679 times in *The Holy Bible*. The form *'word's'* is used twice and *'words'* is used another 543 times! In the beginning, God, Himself, used words to create the earth (Genesis 1:3-31).

Creation of The World Through the Spoken Word:

Day 1—God said, *"Let there be light and called the light Day and the darkness Night"* (verses 3-5),

Day 2—God said, *"Let there be a firmament in the midst of the waters and God called the firmament Heaven"* (verses 6-8),

Day 3—God said, *"Let the waters under The Heaven be gathered together unto one place, and let the dry land appear..."* Thus, The Earth and the seas were formed along with vegetation, herb yielding seed and fruit (verses 9-13),

Day 4—God said, *"Let there be lights in the firmament of the heaven to divide the day from the night...and seasons and the sun, moon, and stars"* (verses 14-19),

Day 5—God said, *"Let the waters bring forth abundantly the moving creature that hath life, and fowl that may fly above the earth... after their kind, and blessed them"* (verses 20-23),

Day 6—God said, *"Let the earth bring forth the living creature after his kind...and God said, Let us make man in our image, after our likeness: and let them have dominion over the fish of the sea and over the fowl of the air, and over the cattle, and over all the earth, and over every creeping thing that creepeth upon the earth...And God blessed them, and God said unto them, Be fruitful, and multiply, and replenish the earth, and subdue it..."* (verses 24-31).

Creation marks the absolute beginning of the material and also temporal world. *"And God said,"* which appears in verse 3, is the first of a series of clearly-defined formula-based sentences expressing the creative commands of God. Creation is accomplished as a result of His words. Each command consists of the following:

An announcement	*"God Said"*
A creative command	*"Let there be"*
A summary word of accomplishment	*"And it was so"*

A descriptive word of accomplishment	*"The earth brought forth"*
A descriptive blessing	*"God blessed"*
An evaluative approval	*"It was good"*
A concluding temporal framework	For example, numbering each day.

In the Book of John, we find Scripture that further supports the supreme power of words. *"In the beginning was the Word, and the Word was with God, and the Word was God."* This signifies the perfect fellowship between God The Father and God The Son in eternity. 'The Word was God' emphasizes distinction in the Godhead and this phrase stresses the essential unity. Jesus Christ was with God in the beginning and will continue to be throughout all eternity. 'Word' means *logos*, which is one of the most important titles for Christ. The idea behind this title embodied God's revelation of Himself to humanity. Thus, God's plan to redeem mankind from the curse of the law was fulfilled by Jesus Christ. *"And the Word was made flesh, and dwelt among us, (and we beheld His glory, the glory as of the only begotten of the Father) full of grace and truth."*

Choose Your Words Carefully

God is continually reminding us, in His word, to be selective in how we speak to others on the job. Our choice of words can build up, but can also break down. Chapter three in the Book of James offers Godly counsel on the dangers of the tongue. In this chapter of Scripture, there are several lessons worth mentioning:

1. The tongue is the primary teaching tool and we can't control it sufficiently (verses 1-2).

2. The tongue represents a system (the world) of iniquity that sets on fire the whole course of life, and is even set on fire by Satan (verse 6).

3. We are made in the image of God. To curse people and yet bless God is inconsistent. Though the fall of mankind has marred that image or likeness, it still exists (verse 9).

4. Godly wisdom is necessary in a teacher for effective communication. The teacher must exhibit a meek and practical application of the truth. You cannot teach what you do not live! (verse 13).

5. Teachers expound two types of wisdom. The one from God is pure and promotes peace, ending in righteousness. However, the other is demonic and natural, visible in the teacher as jealousy and ambition. Results of such teachings are evil living and confusion. (verses 14-18).

"That ye may be blameless and harmless, the sons of God, without rebuke, in the midst of a crooked and perverse nation, among whom ye shine as lights in the world." (Philippians 2:15)

To shine as lights in this world, we (Christians) must be blameless—no finger of accusation can justly be pointed at us— and harmless—morally pure. If we are participating in partying and bickering, as the Philippians were, this cannot be held true. As the sons of God, who live in the midst of a crooked and perverse nation (generation), The Apostle Paul teaches us to be without rebuke. That is, without incurring spiritual damage.

Our proper place as Christians is among the lost. For only in such a position can true witness be borne and influence for The Gospel be effectively exerted. We shine as lights in the world if we remain 'without rebuke' in that we suffer no moral damage by contact with the unsaved. Just as a star is readily noticeable in the dark

sky, healthy Christian lives stand out in testimony among the lost and give credence to one's witness.

"His lord said unto him, Well done, thou good and faithful servant: thou hast been faithful over a few things, I will make thee ruler over many things: enter thou into the joy of thy lord."
(Matthew 25:21)

This Scripture confirms continued service because of good stewardship over a few things. Be a great communicator along the way!

What Type Are You?

"There are two types of people in the world," someone once said, "those who come into a room and say, 'Here I am!' and those who come in and say, 'Ah, there *you* are!'" How different are these two approaches!

Wouldn't it be great to be known as the second type of person? Someone others love to have around? Someone who displays the love of Christ openly, honestly, and unashamedly?

The New Testament of *The Holy Bible* gives us some practical suggestions about becoming the kind of person who demonstrates Christ's love. We are told to give preference to one another (Romans 12:10), edify one another (Romans 14:19), care for one another (1 Corinthians 12:25), serve one another (Galatians 5:13), bear one another's burdens (Galatians 6:2), forgive one another (Colossians 3:13), comfort one another (1 Thessalonians 5:11), and pray for one another (James 5:16).

There should only be one kind of Christian: the "love one another" kind. What type are you? [40]

Final messages of hope and advice on being a better communicator from Graham, one of the world's greatest communicators:

---

[40] *Our Daily Bread*, December 4, 2002

"As Christians we have a responsibility toward the poor, the oppressed, the downtrodden, and the many innocent people around the world who are caught in wars, natural disasters, and situations beyond their control. The Bible has more than a thousand verses related to helping our neighbor in their time of need. Jesus said in Matthew 25:40, 'When you helped these my brothers, you were helping me.'"—Evangelist Billy Graham

"Courage is contagious. When a brave person takes a stand, the spines of others are stiffened." —Evangelist Billy Graham

"Someday you will read or hear that Billy Graham is dead. Don't you believe a word of it! I shall be more alive then than I am now. I will just have changed my address. I will have gone into the presence of God." —Evangelist Billy Graham

FOOD FOR THOUGHT
FOR EXPRESSION

Bill Gates' advice to a high school graduating class at Mount Whitney High School in Visalia, California entitled, "Rules for Life." They are his eleven rules of living—life principles that young people will not learn in school:

1. Life is not fair—get used to it.
2. The world won't care about your self-esteem. The world will expect you to accomplish something BEFORE you feel good about yourself.
3. You will NOT make $40,000 a year right out of high school. You won't be a vice-president with a car phone until you earn both.
4. If you think your teacher is tough, wait until you get a boss.
5. Flipping hamburgers is not beneath your dignity. Your grandparents had a different word for burger flipping—they called it opportunity.
6. If you mess up, it's not your parents' fault, so don't whine about your mistakes, learn from them.
7. Before you were born, your parents weren't as boring as they are now. They got that way from paying your bills, cleaning your clothes and listening to you talk about how cool you are. So before you save the rain forest from the parasites of your parents' generation, try de-lousing the closet in your own room.
8. Your school may have done away with winners and losers, but life has not. In some schools, they have abolished failing grades and they'll give you as many times as you want to get the right answer. This doesn't bear the slightest resemblance to ANYTHING in real life.
9. Life is not divided into semesters. You don't get summers off and very few employees are interested in helping you find yourself. Do that on your own time.
10. Television is NOT real life. In real life people actually have to leave the coffee shop and go to jobs.
11. Be nice to nerds. Chances are you'll end up working for one!

Conclusion

*T*hrough its subtitle, *Called to be **Light** in the Workplace*, this book challenges its readers to be 'light' on their respective job(s) in each of the three phases of career progression: Entry-level (trainee or intern), journeyman level (middle manager), and senior level (executive or mentor). God's Word ministers how to encourage others at work and influence positive change in the midst of frequently dysfunctional employment environments. Through the lives of Jesus, Dr Martin Luther King, Jr., Evangelist Billy Graham, and other recognizable and unrecognizable names, excellence in their jobs raised the productivity level of others. Thus, this book impacts the lives of blue- and white-collar workers. It's systematically divided into three sections, with three chapters each. Supported by the Scriptures throughout, the central theme of each chapter focuses on specific ways to let our 'light' shine and to *Give God the Glory!* while at work everyday.

Focus your efforts, at each phase of your career, on the central theme of each chapter. Each of us has an important role to play to ensure that our colleagues, peers, associates, bosses, subordinates, as well as strangers, know that God is a real God! He resides within each of us, therefore, He is with us at our places of employment. He resides everywhere that we go—Represent Him well!

PART I—The Formative Years...*In the Beginning*

1. Chapter One—Growth
   Central theme: Be open to learn and *grow.*

2. Chapter Two—Development
   Central theme: Develop skills along the way. *Never stop*
       learning.

3. Chapter Three—Maturity
   Central theme: *Responsibility and accountability* are measures
       of maturity.

PART II—The Journeyman Years...*From Learning to Leading*

4. Chapter Four—Applying What You Now Know
   Central theme: *Put into practice* what you have learned.

5. Chapter Five—Become What You Have Learned
   Central theme: *Cultivate your skills* with patience.
       Be fair and cordial as you progress.

6. Chapter Six—What Makes a Leader?
   Central theme: *Service* to others makes you a great leader.

PART III—The Mentoring Years...*Raising the Level of Others'
Productivity*

7. Chapter Seven—Be an Inspiration, Not an Obstacle
   Central theme: *Inspire* others to excel through your character,
       work ethic, and integrity.

8. Chapter Eight—Walk by Faith, Not by Sight
   Central theme: Despite constant change, obstacles and
       unforeseen challenges, *walk by faith.*

9. Chapter Nine—Explain What You Mean
   Central theme: *Be a great communicator* and eliminate all
       guesswork.

*G*lory is mentioned 395 times throughout *The Holy Bible*. It must be quite important to God that we understand how to **Give God the Glory!** which He desires and deserves. As God's chosen children—ambassadors for Christ—we are the visible manifestations of an invisible God. It is therefore crucial that Christians (Christ-like ones) represent God in a manner that is holy, righteous, and distinctively different from what the world wants to teach us. Think about how you will let your *light* shine on your job and how you will make a positive impact. No matter where you work or what type of work you do, always **Give God the Glory!**

WHAT IS THIS ABOUT?

*L*ove. Forgiveness. Mercy. Grace. Goodness. Compassion. Kindness. Generosity.

Who in the world would be against these characteristics, which are common to God's children? Who could oppose such positive forces in a person's life? In other words, who could be against Christians? Who could call Christians nasty names, consider them dangerous, and seek to put as much distance as possible between themselves and Christians?

Who? Surprisingly, many people could. But, why could they? It's because in the Christians they know, they don't observe love, forgiveness, compassion, goodness, kindness, mercy, grace, and generosity.

They won't see Christ and His attributes if we're standing in the way. If we have a self-serving agenda or cause, they'll see our hate instead of our love, our grudges and not our forgiveness, our indifference instead of our compassion, our harshness instead of our goodness. Our lives need to be consistent with the message we proclaim (1 Thessalonians 2:1-12).

Christianity is about Christ and His loving, forgiving, compassionate gift of eternal life. Anything we do that reflects something else gives others the wrong idea. It's all about Jesus. Let Him *shine* through your life so others can see Him. —JDB

*Show me the way, Lord, let my **light** shine*
As an example of good to mankind;
Help them to see the patterns of Thee,
Shining in beauty, lived out in me. —Neuer

LIVE SO THAT OTHERS
WILL WANT TO KNOW YOUR SAVIOR[41]

---

[41] *Our Daily Bread*, March 13, 2002

Concluding Prayer

Dear Heavenly Father, I come to you in the precious and matchless name of Jesus, even the Christ, whose I am and whom I serve. Thank you, Father, for the wonderful opportunity and privilege to write about Your Glory in my life. You are a sovereign God who is in all places, knows all things, and is infinite in power. You are the source of my life.

Father, I pray that through the words of this book, and its message, that you touch each reader and speak to them specifically concerning their issues at work. Teach them how to carefully handle each situation through Your Word. Bless them indeed and give them insight into Godly principles as it relates to their livelihood. Teach them more than just how to earn a living through their respective jobs, but teach them how to live. Your Word says, *"And I, if I be lifted up from the earth, I will draw all men unto me."* Prick their hearts to have a desire to know You and to develop a closer walk with You.

Demonstrate to us Father, through Your Spirit, how to be light on our jobs. Your Word says, *"But seek ye first The Kingdom of God, and His righteousness, and all these things shall be added unto you."* Please continue to nurture and provide for us by continually reminding us that You will take care us of in all situations. Our provisions are cared for and provided even before we know what to ask for. For that, I Thank You.

I ask that you continue to empower and strengthen me to continue to fulfill the vision for 'Writing for The Lord' Ministries and to always use me as a willing earthen vessel. I lift this prayer up to You, Father, in the name of Jesus, whose I am and whom I serve. Amen.

APPENDIX A

Morning Prayer

My Heavenly Father, as I enter this work place, I bring your presence with me.

I speak Your peace, Your grace, Your mercy, and Your perfect order into this office.

I acknowledge Your power over all that will be spoken, thought, decided, and done within these walls, Lord.

I thank You for the gifts you have blessed me with.

I commit to using them responsibly in Your honor.

Give me a fresh supply of strength to do my job.

Anoint my projects, ideas, and energy so that even my smallest accomplishment may bring You glory.

Lord, when I am confused, guide me.

When I am weary, energize me.

When I am burned out, infuse me with the *light* of the Holy Spirit.

May the work that I do and the way I do it bring faith, joy, and smiles to all that I come in contact with today.

And, Oh Lord, when I leave this place, give me traveling mercy.

Bless my family and home to be in order as I left it.

Lord, I thank you for everything You've done, everything You're doing, and everything You're going to do.

In the Name of Jesus, I pray, with much love and thanksgiving…

Amen.   —Author Unknown

APPENDIX **B**

TEST YOUR COMMON SENSE
ANSWERS

1. (a) Cross with caution. This is what you do routinely at intersections that don't have walk lights (and never had walk lights). The present intersection is now one of them.

2. (b) Buy the unfancy kind. You're short of cash and you love all varieties of tuna equally, so you shouldn't spend more for any one of them.

3. (a) The warmer one. If you buy the one that looks much better, you will still need a warm winter coat.

4. (a) Go to the interview. You need a job, and canceling won't help you get one: Your hair will only grow longer.

5. (a) Repair the shoes. They'll be just as good as new shoes for only half of what it would cost to buy another pair. Your financial circumstances are not significant.

6. (b) Don't guess. You have two choices for action. One carries a penalty, and one does not. If you choose the action with a penalty, your score will likely suffer: That's why you were warned.

7. (b) The one with the view of the flashing neon sign. If the question had noted that you love parks, you would have chosen the apartment with the park view.

• Did you know that Marilyn vos Savant is listed in the **Guinness Book of World Records** Hall of Fame for "Highest IQ?"

APPENDIX C

HOW TO BE A GODLY EMPLOYEE
Based on The Ten Commandments
by: Drew M. Crandall, President, Northeast Christians at Work
©1998

1. Trust in God only. Trust in no one but God. People will disappoint you. God created you. He loves you, and has a wonderful plan for your life. He is too good to do wrong, and too wise to make a mistake, even when the "fur is flying." Let His peace abide in you. (Proverbs 3:5-6)

2. Worship God only. Don't make your career, your company, or your boss a god. If you do, you will provoke Him to jealousy and will end up fighting Him. In fact, He may hinder you from achieving what you want until you are broken of the idolatry. (Exodus 20:5)

3. Use God's name reverently. Don't swear! Clean words come out of a clean heart. If your co-workers know you're religious, but they hear the Lord's name used in vain, cursing and swearing coming out of your mouth, you will give the appearance of being a hypocrite. (Matthew 15:17-19)

4. Work six days and rest on the seventh. Before you beg for more vacation time, ask yourself a couple of questions: do you honor the Sabbath? God has already given you 52 days (more than seven weeks) of time off. Are your work, vacation, and retirement expectations realistic, or are you living in fantasyland? By resting one day per week, you can avoid burnout. (Genesis 3:17-19)

5. Respect and obey your boss. You should respect and obey your boss, because you don't know what it's like to be in his/her shoes. Plus, for your ultimate boss, The Lord, serve Him faithfully on the

job, and He will bless you! However, if your boss commands you to do something illegal or immoral, you must make a stand and obey God rather than man. (Ephesians 6:5-8)

6. Protect and respect human life. Emotional, mental, spiritual, and physical manipulation, abuse, and violence have no place in the workplace…or any place. You do not have the right to use and abuse your boss, your co-workers, your employees, your customers, or your suppliers. (2 Thessalonians 3:1-2)

7. Be true to your spouse. If you're not getting the kind of attention and affection you feel you deserve at home, it's common to seek it with someone at work. Honor your wedding vows by avoiding company romances! They are very real, very tempting, and very common. They are also very wrong and are very destructive. (Matthew 19:8-9)

8. Don't take what belongs to others. Stealing at work can take many forms. You can choose to steal materials, money, time, productivity, and joy from your employer, co-workers, customers, and suppliers. Don't remove your integrity by stealing. (2 Corinthians 7:1-2)

9. Do not lie about others. Do not fabricate stories about your boss or co-workers, and spread gossip for the sake of company politics. You're here to be salt and light, not pepper and darkness! Truth always rises to the surface, and eventually you will be ashamed and rebuked if you lie. (2 Peter 2:10-13)

10. Be satisfied with what you have. Contentment doesn't mean that you can't pursue God-given goals…but it does mean that you're content with what He has provided you with day by day. Contentment is a rare quality in today's culture…but it is extremely liberating! Materialism, striving for rank, and discontent leads to emotional, mental, financial, and spiritual bondage. (1 Timothy 6:6-11)

Selected Bibliography and Recommended Reading

A Dictionary of Quotations from The Bible, Selected by Margaret Miner and Hugh Rawson (New York: Penguin Group (A Signet Book), 1990).

Abrahamson, Vickie, Meehan, Mary, and Samuel, Larry. *The Future Ain't What it Used to Be, The 40 Cultural Trends Transforming Your Job, Your Life, Your World* (New York: Riverhead Books, 1997).

Adams, Scott. *The DILBERT Future—Thriving on Stupidity in the 21st Century* (New York: HarperBusiness, 1997).

Amatt, John. *Straight to the Top and Beyond—Nine Keys for Meeting the Challenge of Changing Times* (Alberta, Canada: Kan-Sport Publishing, 1995).

Begley, Sharon. *Newsweek* Magazine. *God & the Brain, How We're Wired for Spirituality*, May 7, 2001.

Bernstein, Albert J. Ph.D. and Rozen, Sydney Craft. *Sacred Bull—The Inner Obstacles that Hold You Back at Work and How to Overcome Them* (New York: John Wiley & Sons, Inc., 1994).

Blank, Warren. *The 108 Skills of Natural Born Leaders* (New York: AMACOM, 2001).

Dobson, James Dr. *Focus on the Family* Newsletter.

Dockery, Karen, Godwin, Johnnie, Godwin, Phyllis. The Student Bible Dictionary (Uhrichsville, OH: Barbour Publishing, Inc., 2000).

FINANCIAL TIMES Newspaper. *Women Who Choose not to Smash the Glass Ceiling*, April 6-7, 2002.

FINANCIAL TIMES Newspaper. *Indonesia Thrives on Peace and Quiet*, July 8, 2002.

FRONTLINES—Snapshot of History, written by award-winning Reuters journalists (London: Pearson Education Limited, 2001).

God's Little Instruction Book for the Class of 2002 (Tulsa, OK: Honor Books, 2002).

Good Stuff, A Monthly Collection of Insights & Inspiration (Malvern, PA: Progressive Business Publications).

Gore, Al. *From Red Tape to Results, Creating A Government That Works Better and Costs Less—The Report of the National Performance Review* (New York, NY: Plume, 1993).

Graham, Billy. *God's Ambassador, A Lifelong Mission of Giving Hope to the World* (San Diego: Tehabi Books, 1999).

Gunther, Marc. *Fortune* Magazine. *God and Business, The Surprising Quest for Spiritual Renewal in the American Workplace*, July 16, 2001.

Harvey, Eric and Lucia, Alexander. *Walking the Talk Together— Sharing the Responsibility for Bringing Values to Life* (Dallas: Performance Publishing, 1998).

Johnson, Charles and Adelman, Bob. *KING, The Photobiography of Martin Luther King, Jr.* (New York: Penguin Putnam, Inc., 2000).

Johnston, William B. and Packer, Arnold E. *Workforce 2000, Work and Workers for the Twenty-First Century* (Indianapolis, IN: Hudson Institute, 1987).

King, Martin Luther, Jr., *I Have A Dream*—Anniversary Edition (San Francisco: HarperCollins Publishers, 1963, 1993).

Laurie, Greg. *The Great Compromise* (Minneapolis: World Wide Publications, 1994).

Leeds, Dorothy. *The 7 Powers of Questions, Secrets to Successful Communication in Life and at Work* (New York: Perigee Books, 2000).

Loden, Marilyn and Rosener, Judy B. *Workforce America! Managing Employee Diversity as a Vital Resource* (Homewood, IL: Business One Irwin, 1991).

Maxwell, John C. *Developing the Leaders Around You—How to Help Others Reach Their Full Potential* (Nashville: Thomas Nelson Publishers, 1995).

Mecum, Shelly. *God's Photo Album, How We Looked For God and Saved Our School* (New York: HarperCollins Publishers, Inc., 2001).

Positive Community, The Magazine, Irvington, NJ.

Pound, Ron and Pritchett, Price. *A Survival Guide to The Stress of Organizational Change* (Dallas: Pritchett & Associates, Inc.).

Pound, Ron and Pritchett, Price. *Business as Unusual—The Handbook for Managing and Supervising Organizational Change* (Dallas: Pritchett & Associates, Inc., 1995).

PriceWaterHouseCoopers *Telecom* Direct Newsletter.

Pritchett, Price Ph.D. *Culture Shift—The Employee Handbook for Changing Corporate Culture* (Dallas: Pritchett & Associates, Inc.).

Pritchett, Price Ph.D. *Resistance—Moving Beyond the Barriers to Change* (Dallas: Pritchett & Associates, Inc.).

Pritchett, Price. *The Employee Handbook of New Work habits for a Radically Changing World—13 Ground Rules for Job Success in The Information Age* (Pritchett Rummler-Brache).

Pritchett, Price Ph.D. *The Ethics of Excellence* (Dallas: Pritchett & Associates, Inc.).

RBC Ministries, *Our Daily Bread*—For Personal and Family Devotions.

Schmidt, Michael A. *Tired of Being Tired, Overcoming Chronic Fatigue & Low Energy* (Berkeley, CA: Frog, Ltd., 1995).

September 11—A Testimony (London: Pearson Education Limited, 2002).

Strong, James. *Strong's Exhaustive Concordance of The Bible* (Peabody, MA: Hendrickson Publishers).

The Holy Bible, The New Open Bible Study Edition, King James Version Study Bible (Nashville, TN: Thomas Nelson Publishers, 1990).

The King James Study Bible, King James Version (Nashville, TN: Thomas Nelson Publishers).

Time Magazine—Special Collector's Edition. *Great Discoveries, An Amazing Journey Through Space and Time* (New York: Time Books, 2001).

The Sunday Star-Ledger Newspaper.

The Wall Street Journal Newspaper.

USA Today Newspaper.

U.S. News & World Report. *Traffic, How it's Changing Life in America,* May 28, 2001.

U.S. News & World Report. *A Christian Dynasty—How Billy Graham's Kids are Firing Up His Crusade*, December 23, 2002.

U.S. News & World Report. *Who We Were, Who We Are, How an Epic Century Changed a Nation,* August 6, 2001.

Vines, W.E., Unger, Merrill F., White, William, Jr. *Complete Expository Dictionary of Old and New Testament Words* (Nashville, TN: Thomas Nelson Publishers, 1984, 1996).

Welch, Jack with Robert Slater. *Get Better or Get Beaten, 29 Leadership Secrets from GE's Jack Welch* (New York: McGraw-Hill Companies, 2001).

What Would Jesus Do? (Uhrichsville, OH: Barbour Publishing, Inc.).

Zander, Rosamund Stone and Benjamin. *The Art of Possibility, Transforming Professional and Personal Life* (Boston: Harvard Business School Press, 2000).

About the Author

Kevin is the eldest son of Ernest and the late Adele Johnson. Raised in Richmond, Virginia, he attended and graduated from Richmond Public Schools and Virginia Commonwealth University.

Kevin confessed Jesus Christ as his personal Lord and Savior on May 2, 1993 during the 11:00 A.M. church service, alongside his wife Gail. Kevin and Gail were married slightly less than two months prior to this spiritual transformation and today are the proud parents of three sons, Kevin, Christopher, and Cameron. They joined that same church and commenced their ministerial service with Holy Communion on the same day.

They currently reside in Clarksville, Maryland. Through his life experiences as a child of God who has grown into a man, husband, father, ministry leader, author, executive, traveler, and speaker, he can attest that *"God uses ordinary people to accomplish extraordinary things!"*

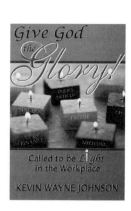

"This then is the message which we have heard of him, and declare unto you, that God is light, and in him is no darkness at all." (1 John 1:5)

Amen.